Into the Wind

Into the Wind

Contemporary Stories in English

Selected and introduced by Barrie Wade

Nelson

First published in 1988 by:
E. J. Arnold and Son Ltd

Second edition published in 1990 by:
Thomas Nelson and Sons Ltd
Delta Place
27 Bath Road
CHELTENHAM
GL53 7TH
United Kingdom

05 / 20

A catalogue record for this book is available from the British Library

ISBN 0 17 432278 X

Printed in China by L. Rex

For my students

Acknowledgements

The editor and publishers wish to thank the following who have kindly given permission for the use of copyright material:

The Lemon Orchard by Alex La Guma, from **A Walk in the Night and Other Stories,** by Alex La Guma. Reprinted by permission of Heinemann Educational Books Limited.

Let Them Call It Jazz by Jean Rhys, from **Tigers are Better Looking,** by Jean Rhys, published in 1968. Reprinted by permission of André Deutsch Limited.

A Sense of Shame by Jan Needle, from **A Sense of Shame and Other Stories,** by Jan Needle, published in 1980 by André Deutsch Limited. Reprinted by permission of André Deutsch Limited and David Higham Associates Limited.

Dumb Martian by John Wyndham, from **The Best of John Wyndham,** by John Wyndham, published by Sphere Books Limited. Reprinted by permission of David Higham Associates Limited.

Samphire by Patrick O'Brian. Reprinted by permission of Richard Scott Simon Limited, © Patrick O'Brian 1953.

Feet by Jan Mark, from **Feet and Other Stories,** by Jan Mark, published by Viking Kestrel/Penguin Books. Reprinted by permission of Murray Pollinger.

A Woman on a Roof by Doris Lessing, from **A Man and Two Women,** by Doris Lessing. Copyright © 1957, 1963 Doris Lessing. Reprinted by permission of Jonathan Clowes Limited, London on behalf of Doris Lessing, and by Simon and Schuster, Inc. USA. Copyright © 1958, 1962, 1963 by Doris Lessing.

A Stranger from Lagos by Cyprian Ekwensi, from **Loko Town and Other Stories,** by Cyprian Ekwensi, published by Heinemann Educational Books Limited. Reprinted by permission of David Bolt Associates.

A Man Called Horse by Dorothy M. Johnson, from **Indian Country,** by Dorothy M. Johnson, published in 1959. Reprinted by permission of André Deutsch Limited and McIntosh & Otis, Inc. USA, from **Colliers, The National Weekly.** Copyright © 1949 by Dorothy M. Johnson. Copyright © renewed 1977 by Dorothy M. Johnson.

I am grateful for the help of all the people with whom I discussed the contents of this anthology, in particular Vron Davis, Ruth Harker, Louise Iliffe, Maggie Moore, Maggie Robbins, John Sheppard and Ann Wade. My thanks also go to Jean Thompson who helped me to prepare the manuscript.

Barrie Wade

Contents

Introduction

These stories were first published within the span of one generation: approximately 1950-1985. They are contemporary in the sense that they are modern and emerge from life and experience in the second half of the twentieth century. But the power of the story is not limited to its own time, nor to the events within it. We each of us bring our own experience of life to its reading. When we discuss a story with others we share collaboratively in the making of its significance for ourselves in our own lives. In this way we can give a story contemporary meaning.

I have enjoyed sharing these stories with students in the upper forms of secondary schools and colleges, and have gained enormously from the discussion of contemporary issues the stories provoke, and from the deeply felt responses to them. I have found that, for those I have worked with, each story makes that special kind of impact that makes re-reading and close study very rewarding.

The collection as a whole also demonstrates the richness and variety of our contemporary world in literature. Each story examines themes of identity, and of the individual in conflict with family, tradition or society. But within these themes, the authors also explore the issues of prejudice, ignorance, dignity, betrayal, honesty, violence, cruelty, tenderness, sympathy, respect, horror, love and bravery — to mention only some of a range of treatments.

I hope the collection will also provide insights for those who are interested in the short story as a literary form, and in the craft of the writer. There is tremendous variety in the story-telling, and an examination of the techniques used by different writers — choice of setting, plot and ending, use of dialogue, realism, humour, etc. — not only helps in puzzling out each story's meaning, but also gives a valuable insight into the genre of 'short story'.

Above all, these stories have an imaginative power which stays with us long after we have closed the book, and this, above all else, makes them 'contemporary'.

As the title of the collection suggests, these stories focus on the varied and often lonely efforts of individual people as they battle against the powerful forces of society, tradition, authority, the family, the opposite sex and their inner selves.

Several of the stories explore aspects of racial conflict. In Alex La Guma's *The Lemon Orchard*, the cruelty and horror of oppression is revealed in brutal reality as the narrative unfolds. The inhumanity of the white captors is intensified by the beauty of the setting and the quiet dignity of their victim.

As an immigrant in a foreign city, the hostility and rejection experienced by Selina Davis in *Let Them Call It Jazz* by Jean Rhys causes a pain as sharp as physical blows. When the overwhelming consequences of discrimination threaten to engulf her, Selina has only her private love of song to turn to.

In Jan Needle's *A Sense Of Shame*, Lorraine and Mohammed seem to bridge the racial gulf between their two cultures. But, their relationship is doomed from the start. Although they clutch at the happiness of love, they cannot be open about their feelings because of the fixed attitudes of both families. The story explores the tragedy of Lorraine's predicament — her ignorance, confusion and shame — in a sympathetic and sensitive way.

Dumb Martian by John Wyndham shows how individuals treat those people who are apparently different from themselves. The story concentrates on the enforced relationship between Lellie, a Martian, and Duncan, a way-load station superintendent from Earth. Here, there is no pretence of love; apart from her inferiority as an alien, Lellie is also a woman and is thus regarded as an investment, a commodity to be exploited by the insensitive and limited man who has bought her. In spite of her initial ignorance, Lellie fights for her liberation in a way that Lorraine (*A Sense of Shame*) and Mollie (*Samphire*) find impossible. Events take a surprising and dramatic turn as the Martian shows she is far from 'dumb'.

In contrast to Lorraine and Mohammed and Lellie and Duncan, Molly and Lacey in Patrick O'Brian's *Samphire* might appear at first glance to be a conventional married couple on holiday by the sea. But as the story progresses, the emptiness of their relationship is revealed and Mollie's unhappiness leads to her desperate attempt to free herself from her stifling marriage and the weak, conceited man who is her husband.

Feet by Jan Mark is a perceptive, witty study of male arrogance seen through the eyes of Jane Turner, a fourth year girl. Jane's interest in Michael Collier is abruptly rebuffed and, although she covers her hurt and exacts a just revenge, her victory in the end is a hollow one.

Doris Lessing's story *A Woman on a Roof* takes an uncompromising look at the way that some men treat women. Three workmen are carrying out repairs in hot weather on a blistering rooftop. Meanwhile, on a neighbouring roof, a woman is sunbathing. The fascination of the story lies in the contrasting behaviour and attitudes of the men towards the woman and her response to them.

The issue of a woman's place in society is also raised in Cyprian Ekwensi's *A Stranger From Lagos*. Lilian is trapped by both social convention, which prevents her from speaking to a stranger in public unless she is prepared for gossip to damage her reputation, and also by her fiancé, who behaves as if he owns her. There are parallels with her situation in the lives of Mollie *(Samphire)*, Lellie *(Dumb Martian)* and Selina *(Let Them Call It Jazz)*. Will she succumb to the pressure of her family and community, or like Lorraine *(A Sense of Shame)* will she strike out for the happiness she desires?

The quest for freedom is at first an obsession of the central character in Dorothy M. Johnson's *A Man Called Horse*. It is only after his capture by Crow Indians that he realizes that "a future is something to be earned". The story follows his progress as he strives to rise from his lowly position of a 'horse', stripped of material wealth and human feelings, to earn a place of respect within Crow society.

Roald Dahl's *The Hitch-hiker* is a masterly story of comedy and surprise. An unusual passenger brings his driver into conflict with all-powerful authority. As events take an unexpected turn the wisdom of judging people by speech and appearance is brought into question.

Liam O'Flaherty's *The Sniper* presents a divided society caught up in the conflict of civil war. Two men stalk each other on the rooftops of Dublin, each convinced that the other is an enemy. It is only after one is killed that the dreadful irony of their relationship is revealed.

Flight by Doris Lessing also explores the theme of conflict, within the family, between generations. The old man resents the fact that his granddaughter, Alice, has grown up, and dreads the day when she will leave the family home. His fear makes him spiteful and fuels his desire to keep her captive, like his pet pigeons. The inevitable pain of changing relationships is a central issue as the grandfather comes to realize the true beauty of 'flight'.

The changes and conflict within the family, so dramatically and poignantly presented in *Flight*, are viewed from a more humorous perspective in *My Oedipus Complex* by Frank O'Connor. The jealousy and possessiveness felt by Larry, the little boy at the centre of the story, are serious issues to him as he competes, first with his father, and then with his baby brother for his mother's attention.

Such is the wealth and depth of experience to be found in these stories as the characters portrayed, in their different ways, are driven to struggle 'into the wind'.

Barrie Wade

Alex La Guma

In 1925 Alex La Guma was born into a family already deeply committed to political activity. His father, Jimmy La Guma, was a leading member of South Africa's non-white liberation movement. As a young man he joined the Communist Party and was actively involved in the Cape Town district committee until 1950, when it was banned. He continued to fight for the rights of black people and in 1956 he was one of 156 people accused in the Treason Trial; the charge was dropped five years later.

In 1960 La Guma started work for the *New Age*, a progressive newspaper, and stayed there as a writer until 1962. During this time he spent five months in prison as one of 2,000 political prisoners detained when the government declared a state of emergency, after violent incidents in Sharpeville and Langa. While he was in prison, La Guma read and wrote extensively. A year later he was arrested for his part in a protest strike and detained under house arrest, twenty-four hours a day, for five years. Before that period had expired, a No-Trial Act was passed in South Africa resulting in the arrest and imprisonment of La Guma and his wife. His wife was soon freed, but it was a while before La Guma was released. He was given bail, charged with possessing banned literature, and detained again under house arrest. He continued to write, although his work was not allowed to be published in South Africa.

In 1962, his first novel, *A Walk in the Night*, was issued in Nigeria, followed by *And a Threefold Card*, published in East Germany in 1964, and *The Stone Country*, published in 1967. By this time La Guma and his family were living in exile in Britain.

In 1973 La Guma was awarded the *Lotus Prize for Literature* by The Afro-Asian Writers' Association. His novels and short stories reflect life in South Africa and his radical political commitment. He is at present the representative for the African National Congress in Cuba.

The Lemon Orchard

The men came down between two long, regular rows of trees. The winter had not passed completely and there was a chill in the air; and the moon was hidden behind long, high parallels of cloud which hung like suspended streamers of dirty cotton wool in the sky. All of the men but one wore thick clothes against the coolness of the night. The night and earth was cold and damp, and the shoes of the men sank into the soil and left exact, ridged foot prints, but they could not be seen in the dark.

One of the men walked ahead holding a small cycle lantern that worked from a battery, leading the way down the avenue of trees while the others came behind in the dark. The night close around was quiet now that the crickets had stopped their small noises, but far out others that did not feel the presence of the men continued the monotonous creek-creek-creek. Somewhere, even further, a dog started barking in short high yaps, and then stopped abruptly. The men were walking through an orchard of lemons and the sharp, bitter-sweet citrus smell hung gently on the night air.

'Do not go so fast,' the man who brought up the rear of the party called to the man with the lantern. 'It's as dark as a kaffir's soul here at the back.'

He called softly, as if the darkness demanded silence. He was a big man and wore khaki trousers and laced-up riding boots, and an old shooting jacket with leather patches on the right breast and the elbows.

The shotgun was loaded. In the dark this man's face was invisible except for a blur of shadowed hollows and lighter crags. Although he walked in the rear he was the leader of the party. The lantern-bearer slowed down for the rest to catch up with him.

'It's cold, too, Oom,' another man said.

'Cold?' the man with the shotgun asked, speaking with sarcasm.

'Are you colder than this verdomte hotnot, here?' And he gestured in the dark with the muzzle of the gun at the man who stumbled along in their midst and who was the only one not warmly dressed.

This man wore trousers and a raincoat which they had allowed him to pull on over his pyjamas when they had taken him from his lodgings, and he shivered now with chill, clenching his teeth to prevent them from chattering. He had not been given time to tie his shoes and the metal-covered ends of the laces clicked as he moved.

'Are you cold, hotnot?' the man with the light jeered.

The coloured man did not reply. He was afraid, but his fear was mixed with a stubbornness which forbade him to answer them.

'He is not cold,' the fifth man in the party said. 'He is shivering with fear. Is it not so, hotnot?'

The coloured man said nothing, but stared ahead of himself into the half-light made by the small lantern. He could see the silhouette of the man who carried the light, but he did not want to look at the two who flanked him, the one who had complained of the cold, and the one who had spoken of his fear. They each carried a sjambok and every now and then one of them slapped a corduroyed leg with his.

'He is dumb also,' the one who had spoken last chuckled.

'No, Andries. Wait a minute,' the leader who carried the shotgun said, and they all stopped between the row of trees. The man with the lantern turned and put the light on the rest of the party.

'What is it?' he asked.

'Wag'n oomblikkie. Wait a moment,' the leader said, speaking with forced casualness. 'He is not dumb. He is a slim hotnot; one of those educated bushmen. Listen, hotnot,' he addressed the coloured man, speaking angrily now. 'When a baas speaks to you, you answer him. Do you hear?' The coloured man's wrists were tied behind him with a riem and the leader brought the muzzle of the shotgun down, pressing it hard into the small of the man's back above where the wrists met. 'Do you hear, hotnot? Answer me or I will shoot a hole through your spine.'

The bound man felt the hard round metal of the gun muzzle through the loose raincoat and clenched his teeth. He was cold and tried to prevent himself from shivering in case it should be mistaken for cowardice. He heard the small metallic noise as the man with the gun thumbed back the hammer of the shotgun. In spite of the cold little drops of sweat began to form on his upper lip under the overnight stubble.

'For God's sake, don't shoot him,' the man with the light said, laughing a little nervously. 'We don't want to be involved in any murder.'

'What are you saying, man?' the leader asked. Now with the beam of the battery-lamp on his face the shadows in it were washed away to reveal the mass of tiny wrinkled and deep creases which covered the red-clay complexion of his face like the myriad lines which indicate rivers, streams, roads and railways on a map. They wound around the ridges of his chin and climbed the sharp range of his nose and the peaks of his chin and cheekbones, and his eyes were hard and blue like two frozen lakes.

'This is mos a slim hotnot,' he said again. 'A teacher in a school for which we pay. He lives off our sweat, and he had the audacity to be cheeky and uncivilized towards a minister of our church and no hotnot will be cheeky to a white man while I live.'

'Ja, man,' the lantern-bearer agreed. 'But we are going to deal with him. There is no necessity to shoot him. We don't want that kind of trouble.'

'I will shoot whatever hotnot or kaffir I desire, and see me get into trouble over it. I demand respect from these donders. Let them answer when they're spoken to.'

He jabbed the muzzle suddenly into the coloured man's back so that he stumbled struggling to keep his balance. 'Do you hear, jong? Did I not speak to you?' The man who had jeered about the prisoner's fear stepped up then, and hit him in the face, striking him on a cheekbone with the clenched fist which still held the sjambok. He was angry over the delay and wanted the man to submit so that they could proceed. 'Listen you hotnot bastard,' he said loudly. 'Why don't you answer?'

The man stumbled, caught himself and stood in the rambling shadow of one of the lemon trees. The lantern-light swung on him and he looked away from the centre of the beam. He was afraid the leader would shoot him in anger and he had no wish to die. He straightened up and looked away from them.

'Well?' demanded the man who had struck him.

'Yes, baas,' the bound man said, speaking with a mixture of dignity and contempt which was missed by those who surrounded him.

'Yes there,' the man with the light said. 'You could save yourself trouble. Next time you will remember. Now let us get on.' The lantern swung forward again and he walked ahead. The leader shoved their

18

prisoner on with the muzzle of the shotgun, and he stumbled after the bobbing lantern with the other men on each side of him.

'The amazing thing about it is that this bliksem should have taken the principal, and the meester of the church before the magistrate and demand payment for the hiding they gave him for being cheeky to them,' the leader said to all in general. 'This verdomte hotnot. I have never heard of such a thing in all my born days.'

'Well, we will give him a better hiding,' the man, Andries said. 'This time we will teach him a lesson, Oom. He won't demand damages from anybody when we're done with him.'

'And afterwards he won't be seen around here again. He will pack his things and go and live in the city where they're not so particular about the dignity of the volk. Do you hear, hotnot?' This time they were not concerned about receiving a reply but the leader went on, saying, 'We don't want any educated hottentots in our town.'

'Neither black Englishmen,' added one of the others.

The dog started barking again at the farm house which was invisible on the dark hillside at the other end of the little valley. 'It's that Jagter,' the man with the lantern said. 'I wonder what bothers him. He is a good watchdog. I offered Meneer Marais five pounds for that dog, but he won't sell. I would like to have a dog like that. I would take great care of such a dog.'

The blackness of the night crouched over the orchard and the leaves rustled with a harsh whispering that was inconsistent with the pleasant scent of the lemons. The chill in the air had increased, and far-off the creek-creek-creek of the crickets blended into solid strips of high-pitched sound. Then the moon came from behind the banks of cloud and its white light touched the leaves with wet silver, and the perfume of lemons seemed to grow stronger, as if the juice was being crushed from them.

They walked a little way further in the moonlight and the man with the lantern said, 'This is as good a place as any, Oom.'

They had come into a wide gap in the orchard, a small amphitheatre surrounded by fragrant growth, and they all stopped within it. The moonlight clung for a while to the leaves and the angled branches, so that along their tips and edges the moisture gleamed with the quivering shine of scattered quicksilver.

Alex La Guma

19

Jean Rhys

Jean Rhys was born in 1894 at Roseau on the island of Dominica in the West Indies. Her mother was a Creole and her father a doctor of Welsh descent. She came to England as a schoolgirl and attended the Perse School for Girls in Cambridge for a brief period. Later she went to the Academy of Dramatic Art, after which she became an actress working as a chorus girl and a film extra. During the First World War she worked as a voluntary cook.

In 1919 she left Britain to live in Paris with her first husband Jean Lenglet, where she began to write. She was encouraged in this ambition by her friend and patron, Ford Maddox Ford, who wrote a preface to her first book of short stories, *The Left Bank*, published in 1927. Her novels were praised, but were not a great popular success, and after the publication of *Good Morning, Midnight*, in 1939, little if anything was heard of her work for over twenty years. During this time she returned to England to live in the West Country.

In 1966 Jean Rhys published *Wide Sargasso Sea*, a novel set in Dominica and Jamaica in the 1830s, which tells the story of the first Mrs. Rochester, the mad wife in Charlotte Bronte's *Jane Eyre*. This novel won the *Royal Society Literature Award* and the *WH Smith Award*. It also brought her writing back to the public eye and instigated a re-publication of her earlier fiction. In the same year she was made a Fellow of the Royal Society of Literature.

In 1968 a collection of short stories, *Tigers Are Better Looking*, was published, including the story *Let Them Call It Jazz*. Her final collection of short stories, *Sleep It Off Lady*, appeared in 1976. Two years later she was awarded a CBE.

Jean Rhys died in 1979 aged eighty-four.

Let Them Call It Jazz

One bright Sunday morning in July I have trouble with my Notting Hill landlord because he ask for a month's rent in advance. He tell me this after I live there since winter, settling up every week without fail. I have no job at the time, and if I give the money he want there's not much left. So I refuse. The man drunk already at that early hour, and he abuse me — all talk, he can't frighten me. But his wife is a bad one — now she walk in my room and say she must have cash. When I tell her no, she give my suitcase one kick and it burst open. My best dress fall out, then she laugh and give another kick. She say month in advance is usual, and if I can't pay find somewhere else.

Don't talk to me about London. Plenty people there have heart like stone. Any complaint — the answer is 'prove it'. But if nobody see and bear witness for me, how to prove anything? So I pack up and leave, I think better not have dealings with that woman. She too cunning, and Satan don't lie worse.

I walk about till a place nearby is open where I can have coffee and a sandwich. There I start talking to a man at my table. He talk to me already, I know him, but I don't know his name. After a while he ask, 'What's the matter? Anything wrong?' and when I tell him my trouble he say I can use an empty flat he own till I have time to look around.

This man is not at all like most English people. He see very quick, and he decide very quick. English people take long time to decide — you three-quarter dead before they make up their mind about you. Too besides, he speak very matter of fact, as if it's nothing. He speak as if he realize well what it is to live like I do — that's why I accept and go.

He tell me somebody occupy the flat till last week, so I find everything all right, and he tell me how to get there — three-quarters of an hour from Victoria Station, up a steep hill, turn left, and I can't mistake the house. He give me the keys and an envelope with a telephone number on the back. Underneath is written 'After 6 p.m. ask for Mr Sims.'

In the train that evening I think myself lucky, for to walk about London on a Sunday with nowhere to go — that take the heart out of you.

I find the place and the bedroom of the downstairs flat is nicely furnished — two looking glass, wardrobe, chest of drawers, sheets, everything. It smell of jasmine scent, but it smell strong of damp too.

I open the door opposite and there's a table, a couple chairs, a gas stove and a cupboard, but this room so big it look empty. When I pull the blind up I notice the paper peeling off and mushrooms growing on the walls — you never see such a thing.

The bathroom the same, all the taps rusty. I leave the two other rooms and make up the bed. Then I listen, but I can't hear one sound. Nobody come in, nobody go out of that house. I lie awake for a long time, then I decide not to stay and in the morning I start to get ready quickly before I change my mind. I want to wear my best dress, but it's a funny thing — when I take up that dress and remember how my landlady kick it I cry. I cry and I can't stop. When I stop I feel tired to my bones, tired like old woman. I don't want to move again — I have to force myself. But in the end I get out in the passage and there's a postcard for me. 'Stay as long as you like. I'll be seeing you soon — Friday probably. Not to worry.' It isn't signed, but I don't feel so sad and I think, 'All right, I wait here till he come. Perhaps he knows of a job for me.'

Nobody else live in the house but a couple on the top floor — quiet people and they don't trouble me. I have no word to say against them.

First time I meet the lady she's opening the front door and she give me a very inquisitive look. But next time she smile a bit and I smile back — once she talk to me. She tell me the house very old, hundred and fifty year old, and she and her husband live there since long time. 'Valuable property,' she says, 'it could have been saved, but nothing done of course.' Then she tells me that as to the present owner — if he is the owner — well he have to deal with local authorities and she believe they make difficulties. 'These people are determined to pull down all the lovely old houses — it's shameful.'

So I agree that many things shameful. But what to do? What to do? I say it have an elegant shape, it make the other houses in the street look cheap trash, and she seem pleased. That's true too. The house sad and out of place, especially at night. But it have style. The second floor shut up, and as for my flat, i go in the two empty rooms once, but never again.

Underneath was the cellar, full of old boards and broken-up furniture — I see a big rat there one day. It was no place to be alone in I tell you, and I get the habit of buying a bottle of wine most evenings, for I don't like whisky and the rum here no good. It don't even *taste* like rum. You wonder what they do to it.

After I drink a glass or two I can sing and when I sing all the misery goes from my heart. Sometimes I make up songs but the next morning I forget them, so other times I sing the old ones like *Tantalizin'* or *Don't Trouble Me Now*.

I think I go but I don't go. Instead I wait for the evening and the wine and that's all. Everywhere else I live — well, it doesn't matter to me, but this house is different — empty and no noise and full of shadows, so that sometimes you ask yourself what make all those shadows in an empty room.

I eat in the kitchen, then I clean up everything nice and have a bath for coolness. Afterwards I lean my elbows on the windowsill and look at the garden. Red and blue flowers mix up with the weeds and there are five-six apple trees. But the fruit drop and lie in the grass, so sour nobody want it. At the back, near the wall, is a bigger tree — this garden certainly take up a lot of room, perhaps that's why they want to pull the place down.

Not much rain all the summer, but not much sunshine either. More of a glare. The grass get brown and dry, the weeds grow tall, the leaves on the trees hang down. Only the red flowers — the poppies — stand up to that light, everything else look weary.

I don't trouble about money, but what with wine and shillings for the slot-meters, it go quickly; so I don't waste much on food. In the evening I walk outside — not by the apple trees but near the street — it's not so lonely.

There's no wall here and I can see the woman next door looking at me over the hedge. At first I say good evening, but she turn away her head, so afterwards I don't speak. A man is often with her, he wear a straw hat with a black ribbon and goldrim spectacles. His suit hang on him like it's too big. He's the husband it seems and he stare at me worse than his wife — he stare as if I'm wild animal let loose. Once I laugh in his face because why these people have to be like that? I don't bother them. In the end I get that I don't even give them one single glance. I have plenty other things to worry about.

24

To show you how I felt. I don't remember exactly. But I believe it's the second Saturday after I come that when I'm at the window just before I go for my wine I feel somebody's hand on my shoulder and it's Mr Sims. He must walk very quiet because I don't know a thing till he touch me.

He says hullo, then he tells me I've got terrible thin, do I ever eat. I say of course I eat but he goes on that it doesn't suit me at all to be so thin and he'll buy some food in the village. (That's the way he talk. There's no village here. You don't get away from London so quick.)

It don't seem to me he look very well himself, but I just say bring a drink instead; as I am not hungry.

He come back with three bottles — vermouth, gin and red wine. Then he ask if the little devil who was here last smash all the glasses and I tell him she smash some, I find the pieces. But not all. 'You fight with her, eh?'

He laugh, and he don't answer. He pour out the drinks then he says, 'Now, you eat up those sandwiches.'

Some men when they are there you don't worry so much. These sort of men you do all they tell you blindfold because they can take the trouble from your heart and make you think you're safe. It's nothing they say or do. It's a feeling they can give you. So I don't talk with him seriously — I don't want to spoil that evening. But I ask about the house and why it's so empty and he says:

'Has the old trout upstairs been gossiping?'

I tell him, 'She suppose they make difficulties for you.'

'It was a damn bad buy,' he says and talks about selling the lease or something. I don't listen much.

We were standing by the window then and the sun low. No more glare. He puts his hand over my eyes. 'Too big — much too big for your face,' he says and kisses me like you kiss a baby. When he takes his hand away I see he's looking out at the garden and he says this — 'It gets you. My God it does.'

I know very well it's not me he means, so I ask him, 'Why sell it then? If you like it, keep it.'

'Sell what?' he says. 'I'm not talking about this damned house.'

I ask what he's talking about. 'Money,' he says. 'Money. That's what I'm talking about. Ways of making it.'

'I don't think so much of money. It don't like me and what do I care?' I was joking, but he turns around, his face quite pale and he tells me I'm a fool. He tells me I'll get push around all my life and die like a dog, only worse because they'd finish off a dog, but they'll let me live till I'm a caricature of myself. That's what he say, 'Caricature of yourself.' He say I'll curse the day I was born and everything and everybody in this bloody world before I'm done.

I tell him, 'No I'll never feel like that,' and he smiles, if you can call it a smile, and says he's glad I'm content with my lot. 'I'm disappointed in you, Selina. I thought you had more spirit.'

'If I contented that's all right,' I answer him, 'I don't see very many looking contented over here.' We're standing staring at each other when the door bell rings. 'That's a friend of mine,' he says. 'I'll let him in.'

As to the friend, he's all dressed up in stripe pants and a black jacket and he's carrying a briefcase. Very ordinary looking but with a soft kind of voice.

'Maurice, this is Selina Davis,' says Mr Sims, and Maurice smiles very kind but it don't mean much, then he looks at his watch and says they ought to be getting along.

At the door Mr Sims tells me he'll see me next week and I answer straight out, 'I won't be here next week because I want a job and I won't get one in this place.'

'Just what I'm going to talk about. Give it a week longer, Selina.'

I say, 'Perhaps I stay a few more days. Then I go. Perhaps I go before.'

'Oh no you won't go,' he says.

They walk to the gates quickly and drive off in a yellow car. Then I feel eyes on me and it's the woman and her husband in the next door garden. The man make some remark and she look at me so hateful, so hating I shut the front door quick.

I don't want more wine. I want to go to bed early because I must think. I must think about money. It's true I don't care for it. Even when somebody steal my savings — this happen soon after I get to the Notting Hill house — I forget it soon. About thirty pounds they steal. I keep it roll up in a pair of stockings, but I go to the drawer one day, and no money. In the end I have to tell the police. They ask me exact sum and I say I don't count it lately, about thirty pounds. 'You don't know how much?' they say. 'When did you count it last? Do you remember? Was it before you move or after?'

I get confuse, and I keep saying, 'I don't remember, though I remember well I see it two days before. They don't believe me and when a policeman come to the house I hear the landlady tell him,

'She certainly had no money when she came here. She wasn't able to pay a month's rent in advance for her room though it's a rule in this house.' 'These people terrible liars,' she say and I think, 'It's you a terrible liar, because when I come you tell me weekly or monthly as you like.' It's from that time she don't speak to me and perhaps it's she take it. All I know is I never see one penny of my savings again, all I know is they pretend I never have any, but as it's gone, no use to cry about it. Then my mind goes to my father, for my father is a white man and I think a lot about him. If I could see him only once, for I too small to remember when he was there. My mother is fair coloured woman, fairer than I am they say, and she don't stay long with me either. She have a chance to go to Venezuela when I three-four year old and she never come back. She send money instead. It's my grandmother take care of me. She's quite dark and what we call 'country-cookie' but she's the best I know.

She save up all the money my mother send, she don't keep one penny for herself — that's how I get to England. I was a bit late in going to school regular, getting on for twelve years, but I can sew very beautiful, excellent — so I think I get a good job — in London perhaps.

However here they tell me all this fine handsewing take too long. Waste of time — too slow. They want somebody to work quick and to hell with the small stitches. Altogether it don't look so good for me, I must say, and I wish I could see my father. I have his name — Davis. But my grandmother tell me, 'Every word that come out of that man's mouth a damn lie. He is certainly first class liar, though no class otherwise.' So perhaps I have not even his real name.

Last thing I see before I put the light out is the postcard on the dressing table. 'Not to worry.'

Not to worry! Next day is Sunday, and it's on the Monday the people next door complain about me to the police. That evening the woman is by the hedge, and when I pass her she says in a very sweet quiet voice, '*Must* you stay? *Can't* you go?' I don't answer. I walk out in the street to get rid of her. But she run inside her house to the window, she can still see me. Then I start to sing, so she can understand I'm not afraid of her. The husband call out: 'If you don't stop that noise I'll send for the police.' I answer them quite short. I say, 'You go to hell and take your wife with you.' And I sing louder.

The police come pretty quick — two of them. Maybe they just round the corner. All I can say about police, and how they behave is I think it all depend who they dealing with. Of my own free will I

27

don't want to mix up with police. No.

One man says, you can't cause this disturbance here. But the other asks a lot of questions. What is my name? Am I tenant of a flat in No. 17? How long have I lived there? Last address and so on. I get vexed the way he speak and I tell him, 'I come here because somebody steal my savings. Why you don't look for my money instead of bawling at me? I work hard for my money. All-you don't do one single thing to find it.'

'What's she talking about?' the first one says, and the other one tells me, 'You can't make that noise here. Get along home. You've been drinking.'

I see that woman looking at me and smiling, and other people at their windows, and I'm so angry I bawl at them too. I say, 'I have absolute and perfect right to be in the street same as anybody else, and I have absolute and perfect right to ask the police why they don't even look for my money when it disappear. It's because a dam' English thief take it you don't look,' I say. The end of all this is that I have to go before a magistrate, and he fine me five pounds for drunk and disorderly, and he give me two weeks to pay.

When I get back from the court I walk up and down the kitchen, up and down, waiting for six o'clock because I have no five pounds left, and I don't know what to do. I telephone at six and a woman answers me very short and sharp, then Mr Sims comes along and he don't sound too pleased either when I tell him what happen. 'Oh Lord!' he says, and I say I'm sorry. 'Well don't panic,' he says. 'I'll pay the fine. But look, I don't think. . .' Then he breaks off and talk to some other person in the room. He goes on, 'Perhaps better not stay at No. 17. I think I can arrange something else. I'll call for you Wednesday — Saturday latest. Now behave till then.' And he hang up before I can answer that I don't want to wait till Wednesday, much less Saturday. I want to get out of that house double quick with no delay. First I think I ring back, then I think better not as he sound so vex.

I get ready, but Wednesday he don't come, and Saturday he don't come. All the week I stay in the flat. Only once I go out and arrange for bread, milk and eggs to be left at the door, and seems to me I meet up with a lot of policemen. They don't look at me, but they see me all right. I don't want to drink — I'm all the time listening, listening and thinking, how can I leave before I know if my fine is paid? I tell myself the police let me know, that's certain. But I don't trust them. What they care? The answer is Nothing. Nobody care. One afternoon

I knock at the old lady's flat upstairs, because I get the idea she give me good advice. I can hear her moving about and talking, but she don't answer and I never try again.

Nearly two weeks pass like that, then I telephone. It's the woman speaking and she say, 'Mr Sims is not in London at present.' I ask, 'When will he be back – it's urgent,' and she hang up. I'm not surprised. Not at all. I knew that would happen. All the same I feel heavy like lead. Near the phone box is a chemist's shop, so I ask him for something to make me sleep, the day is bad enough, but to lie awake all night – Ah no! He gives me a little bottle marked *'One or two tablets only'* and I take three when I go to bed because more and more I think that sleeping is better than no matter what else. However, I lie there, eyes wide open as usual, so I take three more. Next thing I know the room is full of sunlight, so it must be late afternoon, but the lamp is still on. My head turn around and I can't think well at all. At first I ask myself how I get to the place. Then it comes to me, but in pictures – like the landlady kicking my dress, and when I take my ticket at Victoria Station, and Mr Sims telling me to eat the sandwiches, but I can't remember everything clear, and I feel very giddy and sick. I take in the milk and eggs at the door, go in the kitchen, and try to eat but the food hard to swallow.

It's when I'm putting the things away that I see the bottles – pushed back on the lowest shelf in the cupboard.

There's a lot of drink left, and I'm glad I tell you. Because I can't bear the way I feel. Not any more. I mix a gin and vermouth and I drink it quick, then I mix another and drink it slow by the window. The garden looks different, like I never see it before. I know quite well what I must do, but it's late now – tomorrow. I have one more drink, of wine this time, and then a song come in my head, I sing it and I dance it, and more I sing, more I am sure this is the best tune that has ever come to me in all my life.

The sunset light from the window is gold colour. My shoes sound loud on the boards. So I take them off, my stockings too and go dancing but the room feel shut in, I can't breathe, and I go outside still singing. Maybe I dance a bit too. I forget all about that woman till I hear her saying, 'Henry, look at this.' I turn around and I see her at the window. 'Oh yes, I wanted to speak with you,' I say. 'Why bring the police and get me in bad trouble? Tell me that.'

'And you tell *me* what you're doing here at all,' she says. 'This is a respectable neighbourhood.'

Then the man come along. 'Now young woman, take yourself off. You ought to be ashamed of this behaviour.'

'It's disgraceful,' he says, talking to his wife, but loud so I can hear, and she speaks loud too – for once. 'At least the other tarts that crook installed here were *white* girls,' she says.

'You a dam' fouti liar,' I say. 'Plenty of those girls in your country already. Numberless as the sands on the shore. You don't need me for that.'

'You're not a howling success at it certainly.' Her voice sweet sugar again. 'And you won't be seeing much more of your friend Mr Sims. He's in trouble too. Try somewhere else. Find somebody else. If you can, of course.' When she say that my arm moves of itself. I pick up a stone and bam! through the window. Not the one they are standing at but the next, which is of coloured glass, green and purple and yellow.

I never see a woman look so surprise. Her mouth fall open she so full of surprise. I start to laugh, louder and louder – I laugh like my grandmother, with my hands on my hips and my head back. (When she laugh like that you can hear her to the end of our street.) At last I say, 'Well, I'm sorry. An accident. I get it fixed tomorrow early.' 'That glass is irreplaceable,' the man says. 'Irreplaceable.' 'Good thing,' I say, 'those colours look like they seasick to me. I buy you a better windowglass.'

He shake his fist at me. 'You won't be let off with a fine this time,' he says. Then they draw the curtains. I call out at them. 'You run away. Always you run away. Ever since I come here you hunt me down because I don't answer back. It's you shameless.' I try to sing 'Don't trouble me now'.

> *Don't trouble me now*
> *You without honour.*
> *Don't walk in my footstep*
> *You without shame.*

But my voice don't sound right, so I get back indoors and drink one more glass of wine – still wanting to laugh, and still thinking of my grandmother for that is one of her songs.

It's about a man whose doudou give him the go-by when she find somebody rich and he sail away to Panama. Plenty people die there of fever when they make that Panama canal so long ago. But he don't die. He come back with dollars and the girl meet him on the jetty, all dressed up and smiling. Then he sing to her, 'You without honour, you without shame.' It sound good in Martinique patois too: 'Sans honte'.

Afterwards I ask myself, 'Why I do that? It's not like me. But if they treat you wrong over and over again the hour strike when you burst out that's what.'

Too besides, Mr Sims can't tell me now I have no spirit. I don't care, I sleep quickly and I'm glad I break the woman's ugly window. But as to my own song it go *right* away and it never come back. A pity.

Next morning the doorbell ringing wake me up. The people upstairs don't come down, and the bell keeps on like fury self. So I go to look, and there is a policeman and a policewoman outside. As soon as I open the door the woman put her foot in it. She wear sandals and thick stockings and I never see a foot so big or so bad. It look like it want to mash up the whole world. Then she come in after the foot, and her face not so pretty either. The policeman tell me my fine is not paid and people make serious complaints about me, so they're taking me back to the magistrate. He show me a paper and I look at it, but I don't read it. The woman push me in the bedroom, and tell me to get dress quickly, but I just stare at her, because I think perhaps I wake up soon. Then I ask her what I must wear. She say she suppose I had some clothes on yesterday. Or not? 'What's it matter, wear anything,' she says. But I find clean underclothes and stockings and my shoes with high heels and I comb my hair. I start to file my nails, because I think they too long for magistrate's court but she get angry. 'Are you coming quietly or aren't you?' she says. So I go with them and we get in a car outside.

I wait for a long time in a room full of policemen. They come in, they go out, they telephone, they talk in low voices. Then it's my turn, and first thing I notice in the court room is a man with frowning black eyebrows. He sit below the magistrate, he dressed in black and he so handsome I can't take my eyes off him. When he see that he frown worse than before.

First comes a policeman to testify I cause disturbance, and then comes the old gentleman from next door. He repeat that bit about nothing but the truth so help me God. Then he says I make dreadful noise at night and use abominable language, and dance in obscene fashion. He says when they try to shut the curtains because his wife so terrify of me, I throw stones and break a valuable stain-glass

31

window. He say his wife get serious injury if she'd been hit, and as it is she in terrible nervous condition and the doctor is with her. I think, 'Believe me, if I aim at your wife I hit your wife – that's certain.' 'There was no provocation,' he says. 'None at all.' Then another lady from across the street says this is true. She heard no provocation whatsoever, and she swear that they shut the curtains but I go on insulting them and using filthy language and she saw all this and heard it.

The magistrate is a little gentleman with a quiet voice, but I'm very suspicious of these quiet voices now. He ask me why I don't pay my fine, and I say because I haven't the money. I get the idea they want to find out all about Mr Sims – they listen so very attentive. But they'll find out nothing from me. He ask how long I have the flat and I say I don't remember. I know they want to trip me up like they trip me up about my savings so I won't answer. At last he ask if I have anything to say as I can't be allowed to go on being a nuisance. I think, 'I'm nuisance to you because I have no money that's all.' I want to speak up and tell him how they steal all my savings, so when my landlord asks for month's rent I haven't it to give. I want to tell him the woman next door provoke me since long time and call me bad names but she have a soft sugar voice and nobody hear – that's why I broke her window, but I'm ready to buy another after all. I want to say all I do is sing in that old garden, and I want to say this in decent quiet voice. But I hear myself talking loud and I see my hands wave in the air. Too besides it's no use, they won't believe me, so I don't finish. I stop, and I feel the tears on my face. 'Prove it.' That's all they will say. They whisper, they whisper. They nod, they nod.

Next thing I'm in a car again with a different policewoman, dressed very smart. Not in uniform. I ask her where she's taking me and she says 'Holloway' just that 'Holloway'.

I catch hold of her hand because I'm afraid. But she takes it away. Cold and smooth her hand slide away and her face is china face – smooth like a doll and I think, 'This is the last time I ask anything from anybody. So help me God.'

The car come up to a black castle and little mean streets are all round it. A lorry was blocking up the castle gates. When it get by we pass through and I am in jail. First I stand in a line with others who are waiting to give up handbags and all belongings to a woman behind bars like in a post office. The girl in front bring out a nice compact, look like gold to me, lipstick to match and a wallet full of notes. The woman keep the money, but she give back the powder and lipstick and she half-smile. I have two pounds seven shillings and sixpence in pennies. She take my purse, then she throw me my compact (which is cheap) my comb and my handkerchief like everything in my bag is dirty. So I think, 'Here too, here too.' But I tell myself, 'Girl, what you expect, eh? They all like that. All.'

Some of what happens afterwards I forget, or perhaps better not remember. Seems to me they start by trying to frighten you. But they don't succeed with me for I don't care for nothing now, it's as if my heart hard like a rock and I can't feel.

Then I'm standing at the top of a staircase with a lot of women and girls. As we are going down I notice the railing very low on one side, very easy to jump, and a long way below there's the grey stone passage like it's waiting for you.

As I'm thinking this a uniform woman step up alongside quick and grab my arm. She say, 'Oh no you don't.'

I was just noticing the railing very low that's all – but what's the use of saying so.

Another long line waits for the doctor. It move forward slowly and my legs terribly tired. The girl in front is very young and she cry and cry. 'I'm scared,' she keeps saying. She's lucky in a way – as for me I never will cry again. It all dry up and hard in me now. That, and a lot besides. In the end I tell her to stop, because she doing just what these people want her to do.

She stop crying and start a long story, but while she is speaking her voice get very far away, and I find I can't see her face clear at all.

Then I'm in a chair, and one of those uniform women is pushing my head down between my knees, but let her push – everything go away from me just the same.

They put me in the hospital because the doctor say I'm sick. I have cell by myself and it's all right except I don't sleep. The things they say you mind I don't mind.

When they clang the door on me I think, 'You shut me in, but you shut all those other dam' devils *out*. They can't reach me now.'

At first it bothers me when they keep on looking at me all through the night. They open a little window in the doorway to do this. But I get used to it and get used to the night chemise they give me. It very thick, and to my mind it not very clean either – but what's that matter to me? Only the food I can't swallow – especially the porridge. The woman ask me sarcastic, 'Hunger striking?' But afterwards I can leave most of it, and she don't say nothing.

One day a nice girl comes around with books and she give me two, but I don't want to read so much. Besides one is about a murder, and the other is about a ghost and I don't think it's at all like those books tell you.

There is nothing I want now. It's no use. If they leave me in peace and quiet that's all I ask. The window is barred but not small, so I can see a little thin tree through the bars, and I like watching it.

After a week they tell me I'm better and I can go out with the others for exercise. We walk round and round one of the yards in that castle – it is fine weather and the sky is a kind of pale blue, but the yard is a terrible sad place. The sunlight fall down and die there. I get tired walking in high heels and I'm glad when that's over.

We can talk, and one day an old woman come up and ask me for dog-ends. I don't understand, and she start muttering at me like she very vexed. Another woman tell me she mean cigarette ends, so I say I don't smoke. But the old woman still look angry, and when we're going in she give me one push and I nearly fall down. I'm glad to get away from these people, and hear the door clang and take my shoes off.

Sometimes I think, 'I'm here because I wanted to sing' and I have to laugh. But there's a small looking glass in my cell and I see myself and I'm like somebody else. Like some strange new person. Mr Sims tell me I too thin, but what he say now to this person in the looking glass? So I don't laugh again.

Usually I don't think at all. Everything and everybody seem small and far away, that is the only trouble.

Twice the doctor come to see me. He don't say much and I don't say anything, because a uniform woman is always there. She look like she thinking, 'Now the lies start.' So I prefer not to speak. Then I'm sure they can't trip me up. Perhaps I there still, or in a worse place. But one day this happen.

We were walking round and round in the yard and I hear a woman singing – the voice come from high up, from one of the small barred windows. At first I don't believe it. Why should anybody sing here? Nobody want to sing in jail, nobody want to do anything. There's no reason, and you have no hope. I think I must be asleep, dreaming, but I'm awake all right and I see all the others are listening too. A nurse is with us that afternoon, not a policewoman. She stop and look up at the window.

It's a smoky kind of voice, and a bit rough sometimes, as if those old dark walls theyselves are complaining, because they see too much misery – too much. But it don't fall down and die in the courtyard; seems to me it could jump the gates of the jail easy and travel far, and nobody could stop it. I don't hear the words – only the music. She sing one verse and she begin another, then she break off sudden. Everybody starts walking again, and nobody says one word. But as we go in I ask the woman in front who was singing. 'That's the Holloway song,' she says. 'Don't you know it yet? She was singing from the punishment cells, and she tell the girls cheerio and never say die.' Then I have to go one way to the hospital block and she goes another so we don't speak again.

When I'm back in my cell I can't just wait for bed. I walk up and down and I think. 'One day I hear that song on trumpets and these walls will fall and rest.' I want to get out so bad I could hammer on the door, for I know now that anything can happen, and I don't want to stay lock up here and miss it.

Then I'm hungry. I eat everything they bring and in the morning I'm still so hungry I eat the porridge. Next time the doctor come he tells me I seem much better. Then I say a little of what really happen in that house. Not much. Very careful.

He look at me hard and kind of surprised. At the door he shake his finger and says, 'Now don't let me see you here again.'

That evening the woman tells me I'm going, but she's so upset about it I don't ask questions. Very early, before it's light she bangs the door open and shouts at me to hurry up. As we're going along the passages I see the girl who gave me the books. She's in a row with others doing exercises. Up Down, Up Down, Up. We pass quite close and I notice she's looking very pale and tired. It's crazy, it's all crazy. This up down business and everything else too. When they give me my money I remember I leave my compact in the cell, so I ask if I can go back for it. You should see that policewoman's face as she shoo me on.

There's no car, there's a van and you can't see through the windows. The third time it stop I get out with one other, a young girl, and it's the same magistrates' court as before.

The two of us wait in a small room, nobody else there, and after a while the girl say, 'What the hell are they doing? I don't want to spend all day here.' She go to the bell and she keep her finger press on it. When I look at her she say, 'Well, what are they *for*?' That girl's face is hard like a board – she could change faces with many and you wouldn't know the difference. But she get results certainly. A policeman come in, all smiling, and we go in the court. The same magistrate, the same frowning man sits below, and when I hear my fine is paid I want to ask who paid it, but he yells at me. 'Silence.'

I think I will never understand the half of what happen, but they tell me I can go, and I understand that. The magistrate ask if I'm leaving the neighbourhood and I say yes, then I'm out in the streets again, and it's the same fine weather, same feeling I'm dreaming.

When I get to the house I see two men talking in the garden. The front door and the door of the flat are both open. I go in, and the bedroom is empty, nothing but the glare streaming inside because they take the Venetian blinds away. As I'm wondering where my suitcase is, and the clothes I leave in the wardrobe, there's a knock and it's the old lady from upstairs carrying my case packed, and my coat over her arm. She says she sees me come in. 'I kept your things for you.' I start to thank her but she turn her back and walk away. They like that here, and better not expect too much. Too besides, I bet they tell her I'm terrible person.

I go in the kitchen, but when I see they are cutting down the big tree at the back I don't stay to watch.

At the station I'm waiting for the train and a woman asks if I feel well. 'You look so tired,' she says. 'Have you come a long way?' I want to answer, 'I come so far I lose myself on that journey.' But I tell her, 'Yes, I am quite well. But I can't stand the heat.' She says she can't stand it either, and we talk about the weather till the train come in.

I'm not frightened of them any more – after all what else can they do? I know what to say and everything go like a clock works.

I get a room near Victoria where the landlady accept one pound in advance, and next day I find a job in the kitchen of a private hotel close by. But I don't stay there long. I hear of another job going in a big store – altering ladies' dresses and I get that. I lie and tell them I work in very expensive New York shop. I speak bold and smooth faced, and they never check up on me. I make a friend there – Clarice – very light coloured, very smart, she have a lot to do with the customers and she laugh at some of them behind their backs. But I say it's not their fault if the dress don't fit. Special dress for one person only – that's very expensive in London. So it's take in, or let out all the time. Clarice have two rooms not far from the store. She furnish them herself gradual and she gives parties sometimes Saturday nights. It's there I start whistling the Holloway Song. A man comes up to me and says, 'Let's hear that again.' So I whistle it again (I never sing now) and he tells me 'Not bad'. Clarice have an old piano somebody give her to store and he plays the tune, jazzing it up. I say, 'No, not like that,' but everybody else say the way he do it is first class. Well I think no more of this till I get a letter from him telling me he has sold the song and as I was quite a help he encloses five pounds with thanks.

I read the letter and I could cry. For after all, that song was all I had. I don't belong nowhere really, and I haven't money to buy my way to belonging. I don't want to either.

But when that girl sing, she sing to me, and she sing for me. I was there because I was *meant* to be there. It was *meant* I should hear it – this I *know*.

Now I've let them play it wrong, and it will go from me like all the other songs – like everything. Nothing left for me at all.

But then I tell myself all this is foolishness. Even if they played it on trumpets, even if they played it just right, like I wanted – no walls would fall so soon. 'So let them call it jazz,' I think, and let them play it wrong. That won't make no difference to the song I heard.

I buy myself a dusty pink dress with the money.

Jean Rhys

Jan Needle

Jan Needle was born in Hampshire in 1943. He moved to the north of England in 1963, and now lives in the Pennines, close to Oldham. He left school at seventeen to become a journalist, and began writing stories in 1975, having written plays for several years. His first book for young people, *Albeson and the Germans*, was published in 1977. Many others followed in quick succession including *My Mate Shofiq, Great Days at Grange Hill* and *Tucker's Luck*.

Jan Needle's work is varied in content, and appeals both to adults and children alike. Some of his novels and short stores are bleak, dealing truthfully with the cruel reality of social situations (*A Sense of Shame*) while others are light, lunatic comedies (*Behind the Bikesheds* and *Wagstaffe the Wind-up Boy*, for younger readers).

Recently Jan Needle has been writing mainly for television. His achievements to date include *Truckers* and *Brookside* for adults and *Behind the Bikesheds, A Game of Soldiers, Soft Soap* and *The Thief* for children. He has five novels for young children due out in 1988 and has many other ideas in the pipeline. His favourite among his own books is *Wagstaffe the Wind-up Boy*, which he believes children love and adults reel away from in horror.

A Sense of Shame

Although all the lads in the printing works reckoned she was one of the fittest bits they'd ever seen, the strange fact about Lorraine was she'd never been in love. She was quite tall, and put together very nicely thank you, and she had this long blonde hair that some claimed she'd said she could sit on if she had no clothes on — and many a fantasy *that* had led to when the inky-finger apprentices lay in their baths of a night. But until the time she took up with Mohammed, she had quite definitely never been in love.

She wasn't a prude, or anything like that, though. When she'd been at Highmoor Comprehensive she'd been out with quite a lot of the older lads, and she wasn't averse to a bit of kissing in the pictures or at the back of a disco. Nothing more than kissing, true, but even now she was only sixteen. She earned peanuts at old Crawthorpe's printing works, but if anyone suggested she ought to get her kecks off and put her frozen assets into business to make *real* money — on Page Three of the *Sun* for instance — she'd either choke them off or giggle, depending on who said it. She didn't take it seriously, anyway. She knew she wasn't *that* special. Her hair was awful if she didn't wash it every two days and she had her fair share of spots like everybody else. Steve, the oldest apprentice, was the only one who'd taken her out from work, and he'd made a right berk of himself. He'd borrowed his brother's car — a dead smart Vauxhall estate with the reclining seats and all — and after a Chinkie meal in the middle of Manchester he'd taken her for a drive over the moors above Oldham, where they lived and where the printing works was. Quite a nice time they had too, he reckoned. They buzzed around and had a drink at one of those poncy moorland pubs and it was all looking very promising. Then he pulled the oldest stunt of all — he pretended to run out of petrol. She was out of the car so fast he didn't see her for dust, just storming off down Ripponden Road as if she was prepared to walk all the way to the town centre if a bus didn't show up. Steve, it must be admitted, played the gent and went after her. But it certainly ruined his prospects.

Lorraine met Mohammed by one of those chances that happen at work. She'd been the office junior for some time, and after a while, because her typing didn't get much better and her spelling was terrible, old Crawthorpe had asked her if she could add up. He put on a real act of surprise when she said she could, and really was surprised when he gave her some simple money sums to do and she whipped through in a couple of minutes and got them right. Lorraine didn't mind Crawthorpe, although he was a crusty old devil, so she didn't get on her high horse. She smiled and said: 'I weren't that good at much at Highmoor, Mr Crawthorpe, but I were right good at Maths.' When she'd been in the accounts department for a mere two weeks, in walked Mohammed.

She was sixteen, he was nineteen. She was white Oldham and a Catholic too (although the days when the Catholics in Oldham got the nasty end of the prejudice stick are long gone) and he was a Pakistani. She was tall, blonde and good-looking, and dressed in a pair of dead tight jeans and a white mohair sweater. He was dressed in a set of overalls, a boiler suit affair, covered in black ink. He too was tall, very tall. He was dark brown, even for a Pakistani, had jet black hair, and brilliant, piercing, enormous brown eyes. Lorraine's knees turned to jelly. She'd never felt anything like it. She turned away. She *fancied* him.

'Eh, love,' he said, Oldham through and through. 'Is boss in? I've finished that job. Is there owt else or am I to get back to th'works?'

When he'd gone, a few minutes later, even old Crawthorpe noticed she was in a state.

'What's up, lass?' he asked gruffly. 'Are you not reight? It weren't that Paki, were it? He didn't say owt? You look reight upset.'

Lorraine sat down with a bump. She'd often fancied boys before, or so she thought, but she'd never felt this, ever. She'd read about love at first sight often enough, in the magazines, and half believed it could happen — to others. But to her? With a Pakistani! It was ridiculous, nuts. She had nothing against them, but well! Everyone said she was a cracker. She was certainly all right. And one day, she'd always known, one day she'd meet somebody fantastic. But a Paki! She felt right weird. It was ridiculous.

'No, Mr Crawthorpe,' she got out at last. 'Course not. No. Just a bit

41

. . . I've just kind of lost me breath a minute.'

'I'll put kettle on,' he said kindly. 'We'll have a cup of instant.' He bustled about, filling the electric kettle at the big white sink. 'Ruddy Pakis get everywhere, don't they, lass? I thought he might've said summat. He's a darn good worker, that one. Works for Pritties. Every time owt goes with one of presses I ask for 'im by name. Red 'ot he is.' He laughed. 'Well, not by name, exactly, but you know what I mean! Yon black beggar, I say. Old Man Pritty allus gives a chuckle. But he's a reight good little worker.'

Life in Crawthorpe's printing works, for Lorraine, was one big drag. She sat in a small office, more a large box, with walls made of plasterboard and sheafs of invoices hanging from them on bulldog clips, at a large untidy table with a calculator and pads of printed forms to record all the money going in and out of the firm. In a corner was the sink, with a draining board and kettle, next to that was the door to the lavatory that she and the girls from the other office, the one she'd been kicked out of, shared, and next to that the door to old Crawthorpe's office, that he called the Inner Sanctum. Opposite her was the half-glassed door to the printing shed, where the constant clacking and hissing came from and the inky boys poked their heads in every now and again to chat her up. Customers came in through it as well, and anyone else who wanted the boss. Before Mohammed, it had been her one source of interest, wondering who might come in, for like most office girls she didn't have a lot to do, not enough to keep her occupied. She was paid peanuts and she more than earned them, just for suffering the grinding dragginess of it all. Now, it became more than a source of interest. Try as she might to pretend nothing had happened, try as she might to push the unwanted thoughts out of her mind, the door became the focal point of her life.

It was crazy. Before, when she hadn't had an account to do up, or an invoice to sort out, she'd just mooned about, bored but not particularly miserable, rather like her last years in school. She'd read the true romance picture mags that the girls bought on a pool system, she'd done her nails or gone into the cloakroom and tried different ways with her hair, she'd thought about whether to go to the holiday camp at Scarborough with her friend Jackie or whether they should try for Majorca this year — wondered whether they'd dare when it came down to it, two young girls on their own. Wondered, for that matter, whether her dad would let her; he was a right old-fashioned get over things like that. All in all she'd just passed her time dreaming vaguely about things that didn't matter much. She'd been in a sort of limbo.

Now she was totally changed. She was obsessed. She was a horrible mixture of wanting and worry. She watched the half-glassed door like a hawk, willing it to open and Mohammed to come in — not that she knew his name, of course. Every time it opened and it *wasn't* him she felt a lurch of disappointment, that sometimes bordered on anger at the person who'd come in to the office. She got snappy and anxious. And when Jackie noticed it and asked her why, she nearly chewed her head off. It was crazy, she knew it was crazy, and she fought it as hard as she could. Some days she thought she was winning, some mornings she woke up and her mind was free of him, blank, calm. But during the day, always, she'd realize that she'd stopped work, stopped concentrating, stopped doing anything but think of him. And watch the door. She knew somehow that if she could hold out long enough this whole stupid thing would go away, would just fade and disappear. But she wanted to see him. She desperately wanted to see him.

Lorraine had never worried much about Pakistanis before. The part of Oldham she'd lived in since a baby was full of Poles and Ukrainians who'd come in because of the war, who still kept their own language and customs, and nobody bothered. Her being a Catholic helped, and all — she knew that when her dad and mum had first moved in the Irish had had a lot of trouble, window-smashing and not getting jobs and being hated and such, and that had passed away in the end. Then as the town gradually got its blacks, and Pakistanis and Bengalis, you got used to 'em and they certainly never troubled her. There was the odd outburst, naturally, and the National Front nazis got up to their pathetic tricks from time to time, but her dad had fought in the war, and been to Germany in 1945, and the very mention of racialism made him froth at the mouth with rage. He'd seen the camps. When the NF candidate in the local election had come knocking on their door one night he'd almost got his teeth smashed down his throat.

But going out with one, even thinking of it. That was different. Lorraine had this hollow, hopeless feeling. When she went to the clubs with Jackie, or when she was walking round the streets or in Tommyfields market, she found herself looking at them. She'd catch herself out, eyeing up the young lads, wondering at the grease in their black hair, wondering at their leanness and how poor most of them looked, wondering at their cheap thin shoes. The way they talked among themselves in a foreign language, then spoke to customers — those with textile stalls — in Oldham accents, some of them, fascinated her and repelled her. On the X-12 single-decker one day, the bus that went from Manchester to Bradford through Oldham and was always three-quarters full of Pakistanis, she heard a driver being rude to an old guy in one of those funny hats they wore, who spoke practically no English at all, and she got terribly upset. But confused with it. She didn't know whose side she was on, didn't know who she liked or hated. And the idea of fancying one! My God, what did it mean? Much as her father hated racism, she couldn't begin to imagine what he'd say to that as an idea! She knew right well that in his book she would even have to *marry* a Catholic, never mind it being the nineteen-eighties! And she'd look at a Pakistani in the street and think: I don't, it's all right, I *don't* fancy them. Of course he's not special, he's just a boy. A tall, thin, Pakistani boy. Fancy him! I must've been mad! And she'd find herself sitting at work staring at the half-glassed door, find her nails biting into her palms with tension as she listened to the steady clack and hiss of the presses, *willing* one to go funny, to break down. Anything so this tall, thin, unfancied boy would come back through that door.

When he did at last, Lorraine truly nearly fainted. She was standing, putting a bunch of invoices under a bulldog clip, when the handle went, and she turned — she was keyed up like a fiddle string — saw who it was, and did a half-lurch to her seat. She tore the leg of her tights on the corner of a drawer and sat down gasping, red and foolish. He looked worried for a moment, then smiled. 'You aw reight, lass?' he said. 'You look like you've been running. Has th'owd feller been chasing you round desk?' Lorraine tried to smile back, but it wobbled. When he'd gone into the Inner Sanctum she pushed her legs right under the kneehole of the desk so that he wouldn't see her torn tights and tried to pull herself together. She was trembling and she felt sick. She'd never been so happy in her life, nor so miserable. She wanted to die.

Mr Crawthorpe saw Mohammed out of the office, because he remembered how queer Lorraine had got last time. Lorraine had her head down, studying something furiously on the blotter in front of her. When the door closed old Crawthorpe looked at her, said, 'Aw reight, lass?' decided she was, and disappeared into his room. Lorraine let out a long, shuddering sigh. A wave of misery that she'd never known before swept over her. She felt drowned. She couldn't stand it any more. Not more weeks of this. Not more weeks of staring at that *bloody* door.

The door opened and Mohammed peeped in to see if it was clear. A tension like a charge of electricity filled the room. Lorraine stared at him, and although she knew her mouth was open she couldn't close it. His face was tense, worried, his voice unsure, in case he was making a terrible mistake.

'Would you . . . could I . . . like, give you a lift home, like?' he said. 'You know, after work?'

His head hovered in the doorway full of anxiety, ready to disappear at the first, tiniest sign of a sneer. Lorraine said: 'Yuh.' It was all she could get out. A smile burst over his dark face, his eyes glowed. 'Great!' he said, softly. 'Where will I meet you? I've got a spare helmet.'

'Away,' stuttered Lorraine. 'By . . .by . . . Higsons, the chemists. D'you know it?' It had to be away. She couldn't meet him nearer. Well away, well away.

'Yeah,' he said. 'Five thirty?'

She nodded dumbly, filled with happiness, shame and terror. If old Crawthorpe only opened that door! She jerked her head backwards to indicate it and Mohammed nodded.

'Eh,' he said, looking daftly happy. 'Eh, thanks lass.'

The next couple of months were the happiest Lorraine had ever had in her life. A couple of times, lying alone under the pink quilt in the little brick house she shared with her parents and her small brother Frederick, she had a cold, quick feeling, that it was the happiest time she was ever likely to. But the icy clutch at the pit of her stomach passed away almost immediately. She'd lie there, in a glow of love, remembering the joys of the evening, half aware of the sound of the TV downstairs and the cars away over on the main road, and waiting for tomorrow to come, for work to pass, and for Mohammed to be waiting, sitting astride his lovely Honda in whichever secret spot in the town centre bustle they'd chosen to meet.

The very first evening, they'd met formally of course, and they'd kept that up ever since, by an unspoken agreement. Mohammed would wait until he saw her moving along the street, then he'd get off and stand beside the bike with her crash helmet already unbuckled. They'd say hello, almost like strangers, and she'd bundle

45

up her long blonde hair and pull the huge, red spaceman helmet down to cover it. The first time she'd done it naturally, not knowing whether to leave it flying free or not, but it occurred to her almost immediately that it made her chances of being not recognized much better. She felt vaguely shamed by the thought, but she kept up the deed. Mohammed always wore a scarf across the lower part of his face, so that he didn't look like a Pakistani at all, unless you peered close. She never asked him why. But when they got outside the town, sometimes, in the warm wind, she'd let her hair fly out behind, like a beautiful long blonde flag. And Mohammed would unmask his face, folding up the tartan scarf and putting it in the pocket of his leather jacket. That first night they hadn't kissed, they *had* been strangers. But afterwards, when they'd said hello, and Lorraine had got her crash-hat on, they would drive somewhere quickly, not far but to where they would not be known, then stop the bike and fling their arms round each other as if their lives depended on it, and kiss and kiss, and squeeze the love from each of their bodies into the other. Lorraine almost always fell asleep dreaming about that, and woke with longing.

The first night was formal, and although it was a warm night in the spring, they could think of nothing else to do but go to a café. They went to the Precinct, right in the middle, because nobody went there, it was a huge, hideous, empty dump that the council were so ashamed of they'd gone and built another one nearby, to prove they'd not made a mistake. They stuck the bike round the back and sat in a corner of a tearoom drinking coffee and eating cakes. There weren't many other people in and no one took any notice of them, but Lorraine was in a fine old state. Every time she lifted her cup off her saucer it rattled, and she kept her mouth full as much of the time as she could. She kept thinking she must be mad, sitting supping coffee with a Pakistani she didn't even know. But then she'd catch him looking at her, and herself looking at him, and an enormous smile of pure, crazy happiness spread over both their faces and her blood would race and she'd feel quite dizzy. She dropped her spoon once and they both reached at the same moment and their heads banged together beside the table and they left them there, touching. He whispered: 'My name's Mohammed. What's yours?'

When they got round to talking, they talked about nothing at all. Did she like motorbikes? Wasn't the weather nice? How long had she worked at Crawthorpe's? All that sort of nonsense. What

46

schools they'd been to, what films they'd seen, where they went drinking, whose records they liked, did they know so-and-so? There were no pauses, none at all, they talked like they'd known each other for ages. But they didn't *say* anything. Lorraine's eyes flicked constantly between the coffee pattern she was drawing on the table with her spoon, and his face. He had a thin face, with a little black 'tache and high cheekbones. His eyes were enormous, brown and liquid. He was wearing a sports jacket, now he'd taken his leather off, with his shirt collar outside like Pakistanis did, and a pair of good jeans. To her he was fantastic.

She could have stayed all evening, would have done if it had been up to her. But she suddenly realized she was late for her tea, and her mum would be worried, and she had a date with Jackie to go to the Hole in the Wall. Mohammed said he was booked up, too, and they both of them got jealous. Well not jealous, exactly, but worried. She said lightly, but her voice almost wavering: 'I s'pose you've got a date?' He didn't laugh. 'No, I've got to see my mate,' he replied. 'We're in business. Well. We're working on a car. It *is* a business. I'll tell you. Why — are you meeting with a bloke, like?' He said it not as if to say 'it's nothing to me, go ahead', he said it as if to say ' I hope you're not. I wish you wouldn't. I want it to be me.' 'No,' said Lorraine, 'I'm not. I'm meeting Jackie. She's my mate. We're going down the Hole.' 'Dancing?' 'Aye, well. I s'pose so. Not jealous are you?' He looked at her with his liquid eyes, half-serious, half-mocking. 'I might be,' he said at at last. 'Am I to see you again?' It never entered her head to play hard to get. She answered: 'If you like. I could . . . I could . . . Tomorrow. After work. We could go for a drive. If you like. I like motorbikes, me.' They stared at each other across the table, half scared. 'Yeah,' he said.

Sometimes the weather does the wrong things, sometimes it seems to know exactly what's going on and do its best to help. From their first trip across the moors together, for week after week, what in the end felt like month after month, it did nothing to stand in their way. They got into a pattern that grew so strong that it matched their love and somehow reflected it. They'd meet, formally always, after work, and drive away and kiss and sometimes have a coffee. Then they'd both go off home and have their teas. Then Lorraine would go out again — always, if her parents asked, to meet Jackie or the other Catholic girls her father had no qualms about at all — and race to the spot where Mohammed had arranged to meet her. They'd kiss, again and always as if they wanted to absorb each other, become one person, then they'd head off to the moors.

Lorraine had lived in Oldham all her life, but she'd never realized, till she fell in love, just what lay outside it. She'd always seen the mountains — the town lies almost in a bowl of them, except the Manchester side — but she'd never bothered with them. But Mohammed had, and over the weeks he took her by all the routes out of town that led them to the moors. They went up the Ripponden Road through Grains Bar and Denshaw to the bleak heights where you could count over three hundred mill chimneys on the plain, they took the A62 over Scouthead, through Delph to Stanedge and the long drop into Marsden and Huddersfield, they took the fabulous Isle of Skye road up to the heights over Dovestones and across to Holmfirth. They'd drive for hours, not fast, exploring all the small roads and the byways and the little towns and villages, with Lorraine's long hair blowing out in the westering sun which glinted off the brown angles of Mohammed's face. Sometimes they parked the bike in the shade of a stone wall and wandered down to one of the reservoirs that dotted the area, or climbed to a high, windy peak. Sometimes they had a drink in a little lonely pub they'd found. Always they talked, except when they were doing a fast run for the hell of it on a good bit of mountain road. Always they talked.

Mohammed, it turned out, had come to England at an early age, four or five he thought, with his father and two older brothers. All three of them worked in textiles, on night shifts in one of the big combine mills, and because they were older when they'd come in they didn't speak the language as well as he did. They were a lot more old-fashioned, too, in matters of religion and such, and he often got into trouble with his brothers, who reckoned he should do more of what they told him and less of what he fancied. But he'd learned the language fast, got on well at school, and had got an apprenticeship with Pritties, the printing trades engineers. He also had a white mate called Bill, who owned a small garage, and this caused trouble with his family. He was doing a sort of unofficial training with Bill, who was a lot older than he was, and they were hoping to get a real business going, renovating cars, especially old ones, that they could get dead cheap as almost wrecks and sell for a damn good price.

'I'm a natural, see,' he said, as they sat in the sun outside a moorland pub one evening. 'Bill reckons I've got a real feel for

48

engines, I'm not bragging, he'll let me strip down anything. He's —
we've — not got a lot of capital yet, but he reckons we're almost
ready to talk to a bank, set up a small factory, like. Honest, Lorraine,
if we can get that started, the sky's the flaming limit. Honest.'

She was happy to stare into his shining eyes, watch his neck
muscles move as he swallowed his beer. Lorraine felt sorry, now,
that she'd learned so little at school. She sometimes got bitter with
her teachers for letting her stay so ignorant, and with herself for not
having the nouse to realize. She knew nowt, damn all, and
Mohammed knew so much. His factory seemed like a dream, right
enough, but she knew he'd do it, she knew they'd get it off the
ground. She was useless.

'When it's started, though,' she said. 'When you and Bill've got
it going, like, you'll need a girl. I mean, to do the money and that.
You'll need a girl to do your VAT.'

'Eh, kid, fantastic!' said Mohammed in delight. 'You can come in
too! We'll all work together! Eh, that's a great plan, lass! Great!'

They never mentioned Mohammed's brothers' disapproval of his
white friend Bill and what that meant they'd think of her. They never
mentioned what her dad would say if he knew she was going with
a Paki. They never mentioned the future. And when Lorraine caught
herself dreaming, in the slack times at the office, say, or in her bed,
dreaming the normal, ordinary dreams she'd always had, like
marriage, and honeymoons and that, she jerked her mind away to
other things, just wouldn't think about it.

Two nights a week, regular as clockwork, come hell or highwater,
Mohammed went round to the workshop to help Bill do up the latest
'product' as they called it. And Lorraine, because she wanted to and
because she felt bad about it anyway, went out with Jackie. At first,
she'd made up lies about why she was never on the town anymore
— before Mohammed they'd gone out almost every night — even
going so far as to say once that she'd started going to night school.
She didn't quite know why, but it had to be this way. She had
imaginary conversations, when she told her friend the truth, and
they always ended up the same. Somehow or other, using words or
not, Jackie told her how she felt: it was a mistake, a terrible mistake.
Lorraine and a Pakistani. It was such a waste. She'd chucked herself
away. Jackie, who'd been her best friend for long enough, didn't call
her a liar outright, and didn't even get very hurt. She knew damn
well that Lorraine had a feller, and also that the time would come

ITW—D

when she'd get told. The fact that she was in love stuck out a mile: even the blokes at work made remarks about her looking like she was getting enough for three. What Jackie couldn't understand was the secrecy.

One night when they'd been to a club, and Lorraine, as usual these days, had hardly danced with anyone, they left early. Lorraine had suggested it, and Jackie didn't care either way — it wasn't a bag of laughs sitting with a self-imposed wallflower. They decided to walk home, because it was the middle of summer, and the air was clean and warm. Lorraine noticed the mountains nowadays, not ignored them like she had in the past. She sighed as she looked at the long winding strings of orange lights disappearing up into the velvet sky.

'Crikey, Lorraine,' said Jackie. 'You sound like a sick cow. A *love-sick* cow. Why the heck don't you spit it out? Does he beat yer up? Does he give you hell?'

It was a good trick. Worked like a charm. Lorraine leapt to the defence immediately, and Jackie laughed.

'Well, thank God for that,' she said. 'The Invisible Man lives! Honest, Lorraine, you've been giving me the creeps the last long while. What's the big secret? You've got a feller. All right. When I went loonie over Geoff last year I didn't keep you out. What's wrong? Has he got two ruddy heads or summat?'

Lorraine didn't answer right away, just gave a noncommittal grunt. The hollow feeling crept back into her stomach and she felt an aching loneliness. Oh Mohammed, Mohammed.

'What fascinates me,' Jackie chattered on, 'is how you've kept it so dark. I mean, I've never seen you with a feller. You never go to none of our places. And where the heck else *is* there in this dump? What d'you *do* all the time?'

'He's got a bike,' said Lorraine. 'A Honda. We go about.'

'Ee, you lucky pig,' said Jackie. 'When do I get to meet him, you tight cow? Scared of the competition, are you? I promise I'll be good.'

She giggled, because she wasn't half as good-looking as Lorraine. But Lorraine wasn't laughing.

'It's not serious,' she muttered. 'I wouldn't care if you did take him. It's been going long enou—'

They were walking along a broad, badly-lit street by the park. Lorraine had to stop because her voice had given up. She started to cry, loudly, leaning against the railings. Jackie put her arms round

50

her and gently pulled her away from the street light. 'Never mind,' she whispered, over and over. 'Never mind, love, never mind.'

It was a long time before Lorraine could speak properly. For ages the only words she could say were, 'You mustn't tell. Anyone. Jackie, it's a secret, you mustn't tell.' By the time she managed to stutter out she was going with a Pakistani, it can't have been much of a shock. Jackie must have seen it coming from a mile off. She went on cooing and hushing till Lorraine was pretty quiet. Then she said: 'Crikey, our kid, what if your old man found out?'

It was a pointless question and they both knew it. Her parents weren't bad, just ordinary folk, but it was impossible. In any case the question Lorraine wanted answering was different altogether. What did Jackie think? Did she hate her for it? How did she respond to the idea of Lorraine and a . . . and a black? But she was in love, she couldn't really *listen*. She wanted to talk. They went and sat on a park bench in the warm night and she went on and on, telling Jackie everything. It would have been right monotonous if it'd been just an ordinary fellow, but with him being a Pakistani she could tell there was an edge of fear, a little thrill of horror to keep Jackie fascinated. But she still went on and on, she couldn't help herself. She cracked up Mohammed to be the greatest, the finest, the most fantastic bloke in the world. And one thing — it wasn't because she was desperate, no one could think that. All the fellers were after her, she was always being chatted up. It was her own free choice . . .

'Crikey, yeah,' said Jackie. 'You could've had anyone, Lorraine. You could've done far—' She stopped, then said warily: 'Are you, like . . . ashamed, love? I mean . . . Well . . .'

Lorraine would have blown up, but her energy was gone. She considered the question carefully, looked at it from every side, but she didn't dare to actually think. It was a question she wouldn't answer. Couldn't. It was a question that shouldn't be asked.

'You kept it quiet enough,' said Jackie. 'You kept it dark. Eh up, Lorraine, when I asked you a month ago you said you were going to night school. Laugh! That'd be the day!'

'Well,' said Lorraine, weakly. She looked up at the black sky, studded with stars. Oh Mohammed. Her mind was filled with him, she ached.

'Say nowt, Jackie love, you've got to promise me. It's got to be a secret.' She started to cry, quietly, not a lot. 'Oh Jackie, Jackie,' she said. 'I love him, I love him, I love him.'

On the nights in that summer when the weather wasn't perfect, they found another perfect thing to do. They'd drive the ten or eleven miles down the Oldham Road into Manchester, and go to a café in Rushholme, one of the weird and wonderful places there called sweet centres. It was weird and wonderful to Lorraine, anyway, because it was so insanely foreign. Half of the people who ate there were Asians, lots of them in overalls or working clothes, and they had a juke box that played Indian music loudly all the time. The waiter was a jolly, handsome man of about thirty-five who quickly got to know them, and introduced Lorraine to all the sweets of the Orient. Her favourite, which he first called milky sweet, then rasmallai as she got familiar with the names, used to make her shiver with delight, so cool and clean-tasting after a curry. They didn't serve the food with knives and forks — or with rice — and she was shocked for quite a number of times at the idea of picking it up and stuffing it, dripping, into her mouth from a chapati or paratha. She got used to it, though, and became a very neat eater. She never got used to their tea — a cheap glass cup with one third milk and a teabag swizzled round in it for a second or two. And the walls amazed her always. They were panelled, with a tiled picture of an English country scene showing through, advertising Maypole Tea and Maypole Butter. She adored the place.

There were many Pakistanis always in the cafe, and soon they were welcomed as regulars. Mohammed taught her the Moslem greeting and reply, but he always spoke English, and refused to reply if spoken to in any other language. They were a long way from Oldham, and never thought they would meet anyone they knew there. But when they left one night, not a wet one but a fine, warm, loving night, they walked into an ambush.

The only reason they had gone to the Sweet Centre that night was because they had had such a fantastic day. They had both said they would not be back for their teas and they had set off from the middle of Oldham at not long after five-thirty. They didn't stop after a mile or so to kiss, but Lorraine hugged herself close to Mohammed's narrow, black-leathered back. She had on a thin, flowing dress and a very light wool jacket. Even on the motorbike it wasn't cold. The sun was still high, and beat gently on her shoulders. As she hugged him, she felt a rush of excitement. It was going to be a beautiful time.

Mohammed headed right at Mumps roundabout, then left up the Lees Road. They picked their way through the village, he opened the

52

throttle to climb Lydgate brow, and they dropped at forty-five down through Grasscroft with the exhaust mumbling on the overrun. Right and right again over the railway bridge, a hard left into Greenfield, a jog along the bottom of the Isle of Skye road, then the long, winding climb up to the high, flat roadway that led across the blasted heather and peat of the moor to Holmfirth. They raced along there, it was derestricted and empty, except for the odd grey suicidal sheep, then took the exhilarating drop down to the town fast and good. At the bottom they turned hard right and began to climb up the back part of the town, up to where they filmed the old TV series called Last of the Summer Wine, up the narrow, difficult, bending road towards the television mast at Holme Moss. Although Lorraine kept her head pressed happily to Mohammed's back, she switched from side to side to watch the various views as they changed. It was wonderful country, with cliffs, woods, water, moors. At last they were cruising down a long long road on one side of a valley that stretched to their right — not fast, the exhaust popping gently inside her helmet. On their left the moor rose a couple of hundred feet to the skyline, behind them a mile was the huge TV mast, and in front of them, at the bottom of the road, hundreds and hundreds of feet lower, a huge reservoir deep in trees. On the right was a small car park, with white railings, an observation point. It was empty except for three daft sheep as they pulled in.

Mohammed switched off the engine, they lifted off their helmets in silence, and in silence they listened. In front of them the valley lay steep and mysterious, its bottom deep in shadow. Neither up nor down the road was there anything moving. Apart from the occasional almost unheard baa of a sheep there was no sound. If there was a breeze it was silent. They climbed off the bike and stood side by side, holding hands, their helmets perched on petrol tank and seat like big red snails. They drew closer together as they watched the lovely stretch of moor and valley. They turned towards each other and clung, arms and lips together.

After a while, still without a word, they strapped the helmets to the bike, turned their backs on the valley, and walked across the road to the rising moor. They had daft shoes on, thin leather and Lorraine with highish heels, but they didn't care. Sometimes the ground was wet, and they had to jump, laughing, from tuft to tuft of the boggy, wiry grass. Sometimes they held hands, often they stopped to gaze and kiss. Then they'd have to scramble, almost on their hands and knees, up steep bits with loose rock. Halfway up Lorraine took off her tights. They were torn, but she didn't like to litter up this lovely spot, so she hid them under a rock, planning to pick them up later, when they came down again. Right at the top of the ridge, she took her shoes off and left them, coloured like a beacon, on a big flat stone.

Standing up there, hand in hand, they looked at their world. Now they could feel the breeze, and it was beautifully cooling on their bodies. Both were panting slightly. Below, the motorbike was a little toy, the white-railed car park like a handkerchief. They could see for miles. Bare bare moors stretching out behind them, the road and the deep valley in front, and higher peaks across the other side. The TV mast stood silent to their right, towering into the sky, with discs and cones pointing out in all directions. Totally alone, in a small barbed-wire compound, probably humming to itself, but they were too far to hear.

They crossed over the ridge, away from the road, and became invisible. Only the curlews that cried above them had them in their view. The curlews and the television mast. Lorraine hardly knew why, but she took her clothes off, slowly, one by one. She stood there naked, the soft wind playing on her warm flesh, her hair curling slowly round her waist and over her right breast. She smiled at Mohammed over the small pile of clothes. He smiled back, completely relaxed, and started to undress. He too was beautiful, brown and lean, and they lay for ages in the sun, wrapped in each other's arms, listening to the breeze and the curlews, and the sounds of each other's breath and bodies. They lay for ages, with the smell of the warm, sweet grass in their nostrils.

At the Sweet Centre Lorraine had her favourite, meat bhuna, with paratha and a salad. Then she had a double portion of rasmallai. Throughout the meal she sat pressed against Mohammed, and she was glowing inside. It was dark as they turned into the dim little street where the motorbike was parked.

The incident wasn't very violent, but it had an awful effect on them. As they approached the bike, two dark shadows stepped out from behind a van. They were Pakistanis, and Mohammed stiffened. They started to speak to him, brutally, in Urdu. Then the taller one, as quick as a striking snake, stepped up to Lorraine and smacked her face, hard, so that her ears rang and she almost dropped to her knees. He said something, in English, very thickly accented, and she looked at him, dazed. She didn't understand and just stared, slowly shaking her head from side to side. He spoke again, and this time she got some of the words. Dirty trash. Prostitute. Brother. The other man, who was bulky, and shorter than Mohammed, was haranguing him fast and loud, and holding him by the arm. He must have been very strong, because Mohammed was trying to break free, to get at the man who had slapped Lorraine, but he couldn't. There were no more slaps. Both men launched a tirade of shouts against Mohammed, then the taller one pushed him hard in the chest as the bulky one let go his arm. As he staggered backwards they both spat, formally, onto the road and strode off. He looked after them, then came to Lorraine and put his arms around her. They were both shaking.

'Your brothers,' she said. 'Why? Why?'

'They're savages,' he said. 'Monkeys from the trees. Come. Across the road. We'll have to have a drink. I'm sorry he hit you. I'll pay him back for that.'

The Albert, as always, was crowded with Irish and students, and they sat completely private in a corner, enveloped in loud, cheerful conversation. They held hands under the table, sipping their drinks, not talking for a long time. Lorraine's fair skin showed a huge red handmark on the side of her face, which she didn't bother to try and hide.

'How did they know, I wonder,' Lorraine said at last. 'I thought we were safe there. It's miles and miles away.'

'It's a small world,' Mohammed said. 'We've been going there ages now. We should've moved on, mebbe.'

Lorraine thought about that and the thought depressed her.

'Why *should* we?' she muttered. 'We've nowt to be ashamed of.'

After a gap Mohammed said: 'They beat me a couple of weeks ago. I didn't tell you. Not hard, just a warning. Then they said they'd smash the bike. I said that I'd kill them.'

Lorraine laughed, not with humour.

'Kill them if they touch your bike, nothing if they smack me up. Typical.' She said it without rancour, though. She wasn't blaming him.

'I will do something,' he answered gravely.

'Oh, Mohammed,' she said. 'Can't you leave, love? What's it to do with them? You're nearly twenty. Can't you get a place?' She knew all the answers. He was an apprentice, earned a pittance, even then gave most of it to the family. For the others. The people back home. In Pakistan.

55

'I scorn them,' he said. 'Try not to fret, love. I scorn them. They're monkeys down from the trees. Don't fret.'

He did not mention her family's attitude, and neither did she. They sipped their drinks almost in silence.

It was almost the end of a long friendly summer when Lorraine discovered she was pregnant. She sat in the lavatory in Crawthorpe's on the morning she finally gave up kidding herself, with her head in her hands. She didn't cry. She was stunned, dazed. Neither of them had spoken about that sort of thing, she wasn't on the Pill, hadn't the faintest idea how one went about it — and at first when they'd started being lovers she'd got tense and jumpy around when her periods were due in case the worst had happened. But it hadn't, and somehow, inside their love, they'd got to know it just wouldn't. It was nothing to do with them, pregnancy and babies. They were Mohammed and Lorraine. She'd grown so certain, that when Jackie had asked her once if she was — 'you know, all right like that' — Lorraine had said — 'Yes' — so innocently, so unafraid, that Jackie had assumed they didn't make love. Lorraine sat in the lavatory for quite a long time, with thoughts buzzing round her brain almost idly. She'd have to have a test, one of the other girls had done that, it was easy, but she knew, she knew. What would she do? What *did* you do? She shook her head every so often, as if to clear her thoughts. She didn't believe it. It couldn't be true. Not *them*.

Up on the moors above Denshaw, they sat with their backs to a huge rock and talked about it. There was an easterly wind blowing over the Pennines, quite cold, but the westering sun kept them snug against the stone shelter. Lorraine was still more stunned than anything, although when she'd first told Mohammed, as they'd lain in the grass and kissed, she'd had her first real clutch of fear. He had sort of jumped in her arms, given a muscular spasm, and his warm, brown face had slowly drained of blood. When he saw that he'd frightened her he tried to smile, did smile finally, and sat up and placed her back against the rock and comforted her. She could fight the panic, keep the flood at bay, because she was with him, facing more than three hundred mill chimneys on the plain, and the sun was shining. And she still didn't quite believe it. With him it still seemed unreal, untrue. She didn't *feel* pregnant. She couldn't *be* pregnant. Not truly.

But as Mohammed talked, the fear began to creep back. 'What can we *do*?' he kept asking. 'What can we *do*?' And slowly she came to realize that it *was* real, and that neither of them could do anything. He said once: 'But it's easy now? Isn't it? I mean, like, it's legal now, one of them abortion jobs, isn't it?' And she went very cold inside, icy. Because she didn't know, and she knew she didn't know. She knew nothing. No one had ever taught her anything. Mohammed neither, she thought bitterly. And he even had O-levels.

'What about your doctor?' he asked. 'You've got a doctor, haven't you, love?'

The hollow feeling was spreading. She was rapidly becoming empty, vast and empty. She thought of Doctor Whitehead and shuddered. He'd known her since a baby. He'd looked after Mum and Dad for years, since before the war. He'd been there when Frederick was born. She could no more tell Doctor Whitehead she was pregnant than she could fly. Anyway, he'd tell her Mum and Dad, even if he wasn't supposed to. He'd tell them. They'd know.

'There must be someone,' said Mohammed, helplessly. 'There must be someone we could *ask*. There must be someone who'll help us.'

Lorraine leaned her head right back, looking at the high white clouds moving across the blue sky. She'd heard of old crones who did it with knitting needles for fifty quid. I wish I could die, she thought.

'I'll ask Jackie,' she said. 'We'll be all right, love. We'll be all right.' But she didn't feel all right any longer. She felt a deep, blind terror corroding her insides, tearing at her like acid. She could feel it begin to grow, and knew it would go on growing, like a cancer. She was pregnant.

Jackie was a comfort, but not a help. She couldn't take it in at first, just like Lorraine. She treated it like some sort of marvel, like a freak at a fair. She kept saying: 'But love, love, how could you be so *daft*! Don't you know *nothing*, love? How could you be so *daft*!' But when it came down to it, when it came to brass tacks, she didn't know a lot more herself, if anything. She said dead chirpy that she'd sort it out, she'd find addresses and who you went to see, and for a while Lorraine thought she really would, thought it was only a matter of time before something got going. But it didn't. Jackie was as ignorant as she was. No one they knew *knew*. All the other girls who'd got pregnant just got married and that was that. It was all right for posh girls, for students and them that had an education, but their sort were just in the dark. Lorraine floated along quite helplessly, in limbo once again, feeling the baby growing inside her. And the fear destroying

57

her, eating her, corroding her insides.

One day her mother came into the bedroom while Lorraine was standing naked except for a blouse, looking at her stomach in the dressing table mirror. Lorraine moved as if to cover herself, or to hide, then just stood there, her arms at her sides, her face still. Her mother sat heavily on the edge of the bed and gave a tired sigh.

'How long's it been, pet? Oh, you poor little love. Why didn't you tell your mam? Your dad'll be that upset.'

Upset? That wasn't in it, thought Lorraine sadly. When her dad found out there'd be ructions. He'd kill her. He'd knock her head off. He'd kick her out into the street. *Then* Mohammed'd have to get a flat, that was something. But she didn't believe it.

'Nearly three months, Mum,' she said. 'I'm sorry. I'm right sorry. It were done for love.'

She went to face her father quite bravely, later that night, when Frederick was in bed. Rain was spattering on the windows and a draught was blowing under the living room door, lifting the edge of the mat. Her dad, a heavy-set, stooping man, was sitting nervously in front of the electric fire. It occurred to her that he must have guessed already, since her mum had obviously told him there was something had to be said.

He was very uncomfortable, kept glancing at her like she was a stranger. She was, in a sense. It was a right long time since she and Dad had last had a cuddle or a kiss. She sat on the edge of a straight-back chair, unconsciously smoothing her dress down over her belly.

'Well,' he said. 'Well, lass.' He coughed, looked hunted. 'No use beating about the bush, like, is there? Who's the feller?' He added as a sort of afterthought: 'You daft young beggar.'

She whispered in a sort of wonder: 'Don't you mind, Dad? I mean . . .'

'Course I damnwell mind,' he said brusquely. 'I'm that upset I don't know where to put myself. Of course I damnwell mind, you're my daughter.'

She hung her head.

'I'm sorry, Dad,' she said. 'I'm sorry.'

'Ah,' he said. 'Well.' He drew in a long and noisy breath.

'Who's the feller, lass? Is there to be a wedding? Doris! Come in here!'

Her mother came in meekly from the kitchen. She squeezed Lorraine's arm as she passed, and sat by the table.

'Well,' said her dad, to no one in particular. 'Here's a fine daughter we've raised up, Doris. Got herself in th'ruddy club.'

'She'll not be the last 'un,' said Mum placidly. 'Who's the feller, love? Will you marry him?'

'Will he marry her, more like,' said Dad. 'Spoiled goods.'

Neither Lorraine nor her mother said anything to this. It was too dangerous. The mood could change from calm to an explosion in a split second. Lorraine waited. But the question came again, of course. She couldn't get away from it.

'Who's the feller? Is it anyone we know? I didn't even know you were going with a feller. Get told nowt I don't. In me own rotten house.'

Lorraine bit her lip.

'I can't tell you, Dad,' she said. This was it. She paused, feeling giddy and horribly alone. 'We won't be getting wed.'

She didn't have time to wallow in the realization that she'd told herself at last the plain unvarnished truth. The mood was changing, turning to the storm. Her father seemed more outraged by her refusal to tell the name than anything else.

'What do you mean "can't tell"?' he said, his normally deep voice rising a fraction. 'What do you mean "can't"? You'll bloody tell me on this instant, lass. "Can't"!'

'George, George,' her mother half muttered. There was silence, everybody breathing fast.

'Daddy,' she said, her voice breaking. 'I can't. Please. I can't.'

His eyes glittered, on the verge of rage, for several seconds. Then he said: 'Can't means won't and won't'll get you nowt but trouble with me, lass. If you'll not tell me, there's summat wrong, but bugger you, that's all. If you'll not get wed you'll have to get rid, do you hear, the bastard can go down the hospital drain, you dirty little slut. "Can't tell" my arse. You can get rid or get out. You're not having any little bastard under my roof and that's an end to it. Get rid.'

All three of them were shaking, well aware that they were on the edge of a volcano that could blow up in their faces. Outside the wind moaned. Lorraine stood up, her face white and drawn, her eyes huge.

'I'll sort it out, Dad,' she said. 'I'll sort it out. Don't fret, Daddy, I'll sort it out.' She swallowed a sob. 'I'm sorry, Dad,' she said. 'I'm sorry, Mum. I'm sorry.'

She talked to her mother for a long time, later, till two in the morning, with her father snoring in the room next door. She couldn't get rid, she said, she'd made her mind up. The baby was real now, it was a human being. She could not, ever, under any circumstances, get rid.

'But what'll you do, lass?' her mother asked, in anguish. 'He means it, you know, he means it. I expect he wouldn't mind so much except for Frederick, but you know how he is about the little lad. He said to me that if Frederick finds out you're pregnant he'll kill you. He means it, love, he'd do something drastic, I don't know *what* might happen.'

'I'll sort something out, our Mum,' said Lorraine. 'I'll not let Frederick know. I'll sort something out.'

'And *why* can't you tell us who the boy is?' asked her mother. 'Even if he's a married feller or summat we'd get to understand. *Why* can't you tell us, love?'

Lorraine rolled over on the bed and pulled her pink quilt over her face. Her voice was tired, she sounded drained.

'Because I can't, Mum,' she replied. 'Because I can't.'

Sitting in the cafe in the Precinct one evening, the cafe they'd gone to that first night, Lorraine asked Mohammed to do something. Not something specific, but anything. Their hands were touching across the table and anyone who looked close enough, when her coat fell open, could have guessed she was carrying a child. She looked into his dark, troubled eyes, and he looked back, his lip between his teeth.

'I love you, Mohammed,' she said. 'Please. We must do something. I love you.'

There was rain running along the cold empty flagstones of the Precinct, being pushed along by wind. Mohammed's eyes were hunted, and it felt to her as if his hand was cold, as if he didn't care.

'You don't love me any more,' she said, and tears welled up in her eyes. She drew away her hand and pressed it to her face. 'If you love me, you'll have to do something.'

'Lorraine, my darling, my darling. I love you. I do, I love you.'

She waited for the but.

'But *what*, what do you want me to do? What can I do?'

'It'll be showing soon, I'll have to leave home. My dad'll kick me out if he thinks my little brother could tell.'

'My brothers—' Mohammed began, then broke off. She looked at him fiercely, furious.

'Your brothers *what*?' she demanded. 'Your brothers will kill you if they find out you've got some trash white girl up the stick, is that it?

You bastard, Mohammed, you gutless sod.'

He looked at her like a whipped dog. She smiled, surprised by a wave of longing for him, a flood of love.

'They might throw you out, you know! Well they *might*, love. Then we'd both be on the streets. If they knew, if they saw me and knew I were pregnant, they might throw you out! Would they? *Would* they?'

It occurred to Lorraine some nights, when they sat in cafés and the other public places that were the only ones they had to go to now that it was autumn with a vengeance, that if they'd fallen in love at a different time of year, they'd never have been in this mess. If it hadn't been for the moors, and the sunshine, and the dry, they'd never have had anywhere to be lovers! The only private times they got were when the upstairs part of the Sweet Centre had no customers in and the waiter let them sit up there and hold hands and talk. But they didn't go there much, because they didn't know who'd split on them, or when his brothers might turn up again. The only other times they had alone were when Bill had finished early at the workshop, and they'd sit on the back seat of a car being done up, and hug each other in the cold. But he normally worked till well past midnight.

The pressure on Mohammed, she realized, was enormous. She somehow knew it was worse than for her, because she knew he had a way out. They still loved each other, and sometimes she marvelled, almost with joy, at the fact that she was carrying his child, *his* child. Sometimes, for a short while, they were happy. Once, on the moors on a cold, clear, beautiful evening they sat behind a rock and looked at the Oldham lights below them and held each other and cried for half an hour, a strange, disturbing mixture of refound love and loss. As they dropped down Ripponden Road back into the city afterwards, Lorraine felt very grave, as though something majestic and important had happened. They hugged each other when they parted, and kissed lightly, and he left without a word. Better, she sometimes thought, if that had been farewell.

But there were messes to go through. A couple of weeks later when she, desperate, was nagging and nagging in despair that he should find a way for them, save their love and their lives, and their baby, Mohammed broke under the tension. They were in the park, wrapped in jerseys and coats and still not warm, and he stood bolt upright, almost knocking her over, and let out a sort of howl of pain.

'What can I *do*?' he screamed. 'What can I do? Leave me! Leave me alone! Leave me!'

Then he leaned downwards, his teeth bared, and smacked her face, hard, and stumbled off. She heard the motorbike start up, and its sound slowly fade away, and then return and stop. She looked up unseeing as he came to the bench. All she could think of was the slap. Just like his brother's slap. Just like his brother's.

Two nights later he was not at the spot they'd agreed to meet. She phoned Bill's workshop several times from the coinbox three streets from her house, but he said he had not seen him. The next night, when Mohammed *should* have been at Bill's, the message was the same.

Lorraine left for her Auntie Doreen's near Crewe in a black despair that she knew would never lift. Frederick had remarked three days before that she was getting fat and her father made it very clear that he hadn't changed his mind. She'd packed her cases like a zombie, except for the times she'd gone out to try and get in touch with Mohammed. She'd tried Pritties and she'd tried Bill's. Dozens of times. He'd either disappeared, or everyone was lying for him. She behaved as if she'd gone mad. People along the street watched openly from their windows as she trudged to the coinbox, half a dozen times in an hour. She was sunk in misery and grief.

Once she was there, away in Auntie Doreen's semi on the edge of the soft Cheshire countryside, she gave up all hope of him. He didn't know her new address and there was no way he could discover it. She thought of writing to Jackie, giving it, but she didn't dare in case he never bothered to go to her and try to find it out. She just sent her notice in to Crawthorpe's, she didn't go and visit. She didn't want to meet any of them, to feel their prying or their pity, and she didn't want her job back sometime, anytime, ever. She didn't write to Mohammed care of Pritties for reasons she didn't like to face. She felt abandoned and that was that. There was no point in trying any longer, although she missed him with a bitter ache that never left her, not for a second. It was like she'd been in the office in the spring, waiting and longing, aching to see him. She got awful, vivid memories of him from time to time, smelled the warm grass of the moors as they lay together in the sunshine, felt the weight of his lean and lovely body. She would go and lie down, in a darkened bedroom, on her side to ease her bulging stomach, and stare at the wall for hours on end. Auntie Doreen tried sometimes to cheer her up, but usually made sure everyone left her alone. She was very understanding. Occasionally Mum would visit, and Dad did once, but he wasn't very friendly, try as he might. Frederick only knew she was ill, and had gone away to the country to get better.

One day there was a social worker there, a young, pretty girl called Anne, who smoked a lot and swore a lot, until she saw that it disturbed Lorraine. She talked to Lorraine for hours on end and she understood. She'd had an abortion once, she said, at the end of a long and miserable affair with a man who used to beat her up. It vaguely interested Lorraine to find that social workers were human, too. She wished she'd known Anne before. Before it had been too late, before the mess had overcome them, smashed the wedge between them, made Mohammed run away. They had long chats about the future — Lorraine's future, and the baby's, and the family's. She could never go back home with the baby, that was clear. And what sort of life would she have on her own — and the child? She still loved Mohammed, at times wildly, at times with an edge of bitter hate. Would there be a chance that you and the father would be able to get together if the baby wasn't there? Anne always talked of Mohammed as the father, because she didn't know his name. The ideas that she fed into Lorraine's brain lay there, fermenting over the long, drawn out, lonely days. Would there be a chance? It was like a slow bombshell in her mind, it gave her a glimpse of glorious, impossible happiness. Her and Mohammed, Mohammed and her. And no lump, no hateful, destructive, disastrous baby. Just the two of them alone, with their motorbike and their moors.

She didn't know when the word adoption was first mentioned, or by whom. She didn't know whether Anne was truly trying to help her or whether it was just a formula, a simple way out invented by society so that there wouldn't be too many poor, crippled people around. She became obsessed with the hope, rather, that it could work. When she was without the lump, when she was free and beautiful once more, she could go back to Mohammed and they would love each other once again, all the good times would come flooding back. This time she'd be on the Pill, Anne would tell her how. She wouldn't care if they couldn't marry, ever. They'd be together. It was enough. It was everything she wanted. One day she agreed.

Nobody rushed her, that was absolute. Anne gave her opportunity after opportunity to change her mind, at times even appeared to be trying to dissuade her. But as the time for her to go to the nursing home drew near, Lorraine got clearer in her mind that it was right.

One day Anne brought papers for her to read, and she'd already told her mum and dad. They'd visited, when they'd got the letter, and Dad had been a joy to watch, elated. Mum had been happy as well; happy and sad. But over all, it was obvious. It was right. She could go back home, Frederick would never know, she'd get a job again — Dad bet old Crawthorpe would have her back like a shot — she'd settle down. She sat in a chair half-smiling, not really listening. She was seeing herself with Mohammed once more, was seeing the look on both their faces.

As she and Anne sat alone in the living room, Anne puffing at a fag, shuffling the papers, it came to Lorraine that still the social worker did not know: no one did. She looked down at her big belly, and wondered how to start. Ah well, it was a little human being now, almost ready to pop out. Someone had to stand up for it.

'He'll be a half-caste, Anne,' she said. 'I want to call him Denny. Short for Dennis.'

Anne smiled easily, totally unshocked, unsurprised.

'Are you sure he'll be a boy, Lorraine?' she asked. 'Some babies turn out girls, you know.'

'He'll be a boy,' said Lorraine. 'I'm going to call him Denny. He'll be a half-caste.'

Anne eyed her levelly.

'Is that why he's had to go?' she asked. 'Is that why the adoption? It's a sod, life, isn't it? It can be. A right sod.' She stopped. 'There'll be about six months before it's final, Lorraine, I told you didn't I? That's not to say you could change your mind easily, because you couldn't. But you're not allowed to sign a thing for nearly two months, then nothing's final for at least another three; you could fight it. There's about six months.'

Lorraine shook her head.

'I can't change my mind,' she said. 'I won't.'

'It's nothing to be ashamed of,' said Anne, looking at her closely. 'That he's black. It doesn't mean you've done wrong, more wrong than if it'd been an ordinary English guy. You must believe me, Lorraine, it's very important. I know it makes things harder, that you'd get more stick from people, from your mum and dad and that, but you mustn't feel ashamed.'

She thought Anne was going to ask if she'd been right, if Lorraine *did* feel that sense of shame, and she began to panic, in terrible fright as to how she could reply. But Anne just said: 'Do you still love him?

The father? You do, don't you, love?'

Lorraine could barely speak.

'Yuh,' she croaked. 'He's not black, he's a Pakistani. He's called Mohammed.' She felt stupid, she knew it was a betrayal. Had Jackie said it was a waste, her going with a Pakistani, or had she dreamed it? She could have done better, she could have had anybody she wanted. Well this was a waste, a terrible, horrible waste, all of it. Her mind was filled with loss and hatred.

In the nursing home south of Crewe, clean and white and pleasant, she held Denny in her arms, Denise, a little girl, not very dark at all, except for her eyes, which were huge and brown and liquid. She did not hold her long, though, because already she could feel an enormous flower of love inside her, growing, ready to burst and engulf her, and she was determined. Denny was fair-skinned, but not that fair-skinned, and her parents must not see her. In any case, she could not stay. The love was Lorraine's, not her mum and dad's, and Dad would chuck her out and keep her chucked. Frederick would never even know this way. Her illness had been cured. Anne said it was best, and Lorraine knew she was right. She held her daughter once, then let her go. They may have stuffed her full of drugs, for all she knew, because she began to feel woozy immediately, her mind began to wander. A sweet little child, a tiny little baby. As she drifted off, it did not seem to have much to do with her. It never had. She tried to think of Mohammed, to think of love. But his face was blurred, and her feelings weren't real, or clear; just woozy. Mohammed, Mohammed, Mohammed, what was it? What was left?

Her eyelids fluttered and she groaned, twisting her head on the deep, white pillow. What had Anne said? Six months before it was final, six months. She groaned once more. She had six months.

Jan Needle

John Wyndham

John Wyndham is one of the several pseudonyms used by John Wyndham Parkes Lucas Beynon Harris. Born in 1903, the son of a barrister, he attended a number of prep schools before starting at Bedales, a progressive independent school, in 1918. This suited his needs and personality and he stayed at Bedales until 1921.

On leaving school he chose not to go to university (a decision he was later to regret) and instead he worked at various jobs. By 1925, aged twenty-two, he was producing short stories for publication and by 1930, he was writing regularly, sending his short stories (his main output) to American magazines. In 1934 he published his first book, *The Secret People*, under the pen name of John Beynon. It explored the theme of survival and bore similarities to Jules Verne's story, *Journey to the Centre of the Earth*. The following year he wrote a detective story, *Foul Play Suspected*, also under the name of John Beynon. This early writing was characterized by a strong element of fantasy.

During the war he experienced both civil and military service and began to write again in 1946, in a style recognized as science fiction. However, he referred to his own writing as *logical fantasy*. The first book to be written in this genre was *The Day of the Triffids*, published in 1951. There followed various novels and short stories, now well-known, several of which have been made into films. After a gap of six years he wrote his last book, *Chocky*, in 1968.

In later years John Wyndham lived with his wife in a small house in the Hampshire countryside, within ten minutes walk of Bedales. He died in March 1969 aged sixty-six.

Dumb Martian

When Duncan Weaver bought Lellie for – no, there could be trouble putting it that way – when Duncan Weaver paid Lellie's parents one thousand pounds in compensation for the loss of her services, he had a figure of six, or, if absolutely necessary, seven hundred in mind.

Everybody in Port Clarke that he had asked about it assured him that that would be a fair price. But when he got up country it hadn't turned out quite as simple as the Port Clarkers seemed to think. The first three Martian families he had tackled hadn't shown any disposition to sell their daughters at all; the next wanted £1,500, and wouldn't budge; Lellie's parents had started at £1,500, too, but they came down to £1,000 when he'd made it plain that he wasn't going to stand for extortion. And when, on the way back to Port Clarke with her, he came to work it out, he found himself not so badly pleased with the deal after all. Over the five-year term of his appointment it could only cost him £200 a year at the worst – that is to say if he were not able to sell her for £400, maybe £500 when he got back. Looked at that way, it wasn't really at all unreasonable.

In town once more, he went to explain the situation and get things all set with the Company's Agent.

'Look,' he said, 'you know the way I'm fixed with this five-year contract as Way-load Station Superintendent on Jupiter IV/II? Well, the ship that takes me there will be travelling light to pick up cargo. So how about a second passage on her?' He had already taken the precautionary step of finding out that the Company was accustomed to grant an extra passage in such circumstances, though not of right.

The Company's Agent was not surprised. After consulting some lists, he said that he saw no objection to an extra passenger. He explained that the Company was also prepared in such cases to supply the extra ration of food for one person at the nominal charge of £200 per annum, payable by deduction from salary.

'What! A thousand pounds!' Duncan exclaimed.

'Well worth it,' said the Agent. 'It *is* nominal for the rations, because it's worth the Company's while to lay out the rest for something that helps to keep an employee from going nuts. That's pretty easy to do when you're fixed alone on a way-load station, they tell me – and I believe them. A thousand's not high if it helps you to avoid a crack-up.'

Duncan argued it a bit, on principle, but the Agent had the thing cut and dried. It mean that Lellie's price went up to £2,000 – £400 a year. Still, with his own salary at £5,000 a year, tax free, unspendable during his term on Jupiter IV/II, and piling up nicely, it wouldn't come to such a big slice. So he agreed.

'Fine,' said the Agent. 'I'll fix it, then. All you'll need is an embarkation permit for her, and they'll grant that automatically on production of your marriage certificate.'

Duncan stared.

'Marriage certificate! What, me! Me marry a Mart!'

The Agent shook his head reprovingly.

'No embarkation permit without it. Anti-slavery regulation. They'd likely think you meant to sell her – might even think you'd bought her.'

'What, me!' Duncan said again, indignantly.

'Even you,' said the Agent. 'A marriage licence will only cost you another ten pounds – unless you've got a wife back home, in which case it'll likely cost you a bit more later on.'

Duncan shook his head.

'I've no wife,' he assured him.

'Uh-huh,' said the Agent, neither believing, nor disbelieving. 'Then what's the difference?'

Duncan came back a couple of days later, with the certificate and the permit. The Agent looked them over.

'That's OK,' he agreed. 'I'll confirm the booking. My fee will be one hundred pounds.'

'Your fee! What the —?'

'Call it safeguarding your investment,' said the Agent.

The man who had issued the embarkation permit had required one hundred pounds, too. Duncan did not mention that now, but he said, with bitterness:

'One dumb Mart's costing me plenty.'

'Dumb?' said the Agent, looking at him.

'Speechless plus. These hick Marts don't know they're born.'

'H'm,' said the Agent. 'Never lived here, have you?'

'No,' Duncan admitted. 'But I've laid-over here a few times.'

The Agent nodded.

'They act dumb, and the way their faces are makes them look dumb,' he said, 'but they were a mighty clever people, once.'

'Once, could be a long time ago.'

'Long before we got here they'd given up bothering to think a lot. Their planet was dying, and they were kind of content to die with it.'

'Well I call that dumb. Aren't all planets dying, anyway?'

'Ever seen an old man just sitting in the sun, taking it easy? It doesn't have to mean he's senile. It may do, but very likely he can snap out of it and put his mind to work again if it gets really necessary. But mostly he finds it not worth the bother. Less trouble just to let things happen.'

'Well, this one's only about twenty – say ten and a half of your Martian years – and she certainly lets 'em happen. And I'd say it's a kind of acid test for dumbness when a girl doesn't know what goes on at her own wedding ceremony.'

And then, on top of that, it turned out to be necessary to lay out yet another hundred pounds on clothing and other things for her, bringing the whole investment up to £2,310. It was a sum which might possibly have been justified on a really *smart* girl, but Lellie . . . But there it was. Once you made the first payment, you either lost on it, or were stuck for the rest. And, anyway, on a lonely way-load station even she would be company – of a sort . . .

The First Officer called Duncan into the navigating room to take a look at his future home.

'There it is,' he said, waving his hand at a watch-screen.

Duncan looked at the jagged-surfaced crescent. There was no scale to it: it could have been the size of Luna, or of a basketball. Either size, it was still just a lump of rock, turning slowly over.

'How big?' he asked.

'Around forty miles mean diameter.'

'What'd that be in gravity?'

'Haven't worked it out. Call it slight, and reckon there isn't any, and you'll be near enough.'

'Uh-huh,' said Duncan.

On the way back to the mess-room he paused to put his head into the cabin. Lellie was lying on her bunk, with the spring-cover fastened over her to give some illusion of weight. At the sight of him she raised herself on one elbow.

She was small – not much over five feet. Her face and hands were delicate; they had a fragility which was not simply a matter of poor bone-structure. To an Earthman her eyes looked unnaturally round, seeming to give her permanently an expression of innocence surprised. The lobes of her ears hung unusually low out of a mass of brown hair that glinted with red among its waves. The paleness of her skin was emphasized by the colour on her cheeks and the vivid red on her lips.

'Hey,' said Duncan. 'You can start to get busy packing up the stuff now.'

'Packing up?' she repeated doubtfully, in a curiously resonant voice.

'Sure. Pack.' Duncan told her. He demonstrated by opening a box, cramming some clothes into it, and waving a hand to include the rest. Her expression did not change, but the idea got across.

'We are come?' she asked.

'We are nearly come. So get busy on this lot,' he informed her.

'Yith – OK,' she said, and began to unhook the cover.

Duncan shut the door, and gave a shove which sent him floating down the passage leading to the general mess and living room.

Inside the cabin, Lellie pushed away the cover. She reached down cautiously for a pair of metallic soles, and attached them to her slippers by their clips. Still cautiously holding on to the bunk, she swung her feet over the side and lowered them until the magnetic soles clicked into contact with the floor. She stood up, more confidently. The brown overall suit she wore revealed proportions that might be admired among Martians, but by Earth standards they were not classic – it is said to be the consequence of the thinner air of Mars that has in the course of time produced a greater lung capacity, with consequent modification. Still ill at ease with her condition of weightlessness, she slid her feet to keep contact as she crossed the room. For some moments she paused in front of a wall mirror, contemplating her reflection. Then she turned away and set about the packing.

'– one hell of a place to take a woman to,' Wishart, the ship's cook, was saying as Duncan came in.

Duncan did not care a lot for Wishart – chiefly on account of the fact that when it had occurred to him that it was highly desirable for

71

Lellie to have some lessons in weightless cooking, Wishart had refused to give the tuition for less than £50, and thus increased the investment cost to £2,360. Nevertheless, it was not his way to pretend to have misheard.

'One hell of a place to be given a job,' he said grimly.

No one replied to that. They knew how men came to be offered way-load jobs.

It was not necessary, as the Company frequently pointed out, for superannuation at the age of forty to come as a hardship to anyone: salaries were good, and they could cite plenty of cases where men had founded brilliant subsequent careers on the savings of their space-service days. That was all right for the men who had saved, and had not been obsessively interested in the fact that one four-legged animal can run faster than another. But this was not even an enterprising way to have lost one's money, so when it came to Duncan's time to leave crew work they made him no more than a routine offer.

He had never been to Jupiter IV/II, but he knew just what it would be like — something that was second moon to Callisto; itself fourth moon, in order of discovery, to Jupiter; would inevitably be one of the grimmer kinds of cosmic pebble. They offered no alternative, so he signed up at the usual terms: £5,000 a year for five years, all found, plus five months waiting time on half-pay before he could get there, plus six months afterwards, also on half-pay, during 'readjustment to gravity'.

Well – it meant the next six years taken care of; five of them without expenses, and a nice little sum at the end.

The splinter in the mouthful was: could you get through five years of isolation without cracking up? Even when the psychologist had okayed you, you couldn't be sure. Some could: others went to pieces in a few months, and had to be taken off, gibbering. If you got through two years, they said, you'd be OK for five. But the only way to find out about the two was to try . . .

'What about my putting in the waiting time on Mars? I could live cheaper there,' Duncan suggested.

They had consulted the planetary tables and sailing schedules, and discovered that it would come cheaper for them, too. They had declined to split the difference on the saving thus made, but they had booked him a passage for the following week, and arranged for him to draw, on credit, from the Company's agent there.

The Martian colony in and around Port Clarke is rich in ex-spaceman who find it more comfortable to spend their rearguard years in the lesser gravity, broader morality and greater economy obtaining there. They are great advisers. Duncan listened, but discarded most of it. Such methods of occupying oneself to preserve sanity as learning the Bible or the works of Shakespeare by heart, or copying out three pages of the Encyclopaedia every day, or building model spaceships in bottles, struck him not only as tedious, but probably of doubtful efficacy, as well. The only one which he had felt to show sound practical advantages was that which had led him to picking Lellie to share his exile, and he still fancied it was a sound one, in spite of its letting him in for £2,360.

He was well enough aware of the general opinion about it to refrain from adding a sharp retort to Wishart. Instead, he conceded:

'Maybe it'd not do to take a *real* woman to a place like that. But a Mart's kind of different . . .'

'Even a Mart—' Wishart began, but he was cut short by finding himself drifting slowly across the room as the arrester tubes began to fire.

Conversation ceased as everybody turned-to on the job of securing all loose objects.

Jupiter IV/II was, by definition, a sub-moon, and probably a captured asteroid. The surface was not cratered, like Luna's: it was simply a waste of jagged, riven rocks. The satellite as a whole had the form of an irregular ovoid; it was a bleak, cheerless lump of stone splintered off some vanished planet, with nothing whatever to commend it but its situation.

There have to be way-load stations. It would be hopelessly uneconomic to build big ships capable of landing on the major planets. A few of the older and smaller ships were indeed built on Earth, and so had to be launched from there, but the very first large, moon-assembled ship established a new practice. Ships became truly *space*ships and were no longer built to stand the strains of high gravitational pull. They began to make their voyages, carrying fuel, stores, freight and changes of personnel, exclusively between satellites. Newer types do not put in even at Luna, but use the artificial satellite, Pseudos, exclusively as their Earth terminus.

Freight between the way-loads and their primaries is customarily consigned in powered cylinders known as crates; passengers are ferried back and forth in small rocketships. Stations such as Pseudos, or Deimos, the main way-load for Mars, handle enough work to keep a crew busy, but in the outlying, little-developed posts one man who is part-handler, part-watchman is enough. Ships visited them infrequently. On Jupiter IV/II one might, according to Duncan's information, expect an average of one every eight or nine months (Earth).

The ship continued to slow, coming in on a spiral, adjusting her speed to that of the satellite. The gyros started up to give stability. The small, jagged world grew until it overflowed the watch-screens. The ship was manoeuvred into a close orbit. Miles of featureless, formidable rocks slid monotonously beneath her.

The station site came sliding on to the screen from the left; a roughly levelled area of a few acres; the first and only sign of order in the stony chaos. At the far end was a pair of hemispherical huts, one much larger than the other. At the near end, a few cylindrical crates were lined up beside a launching ramp hewn from the rock. Down each side of the area stood rows of canvas bins, some stuffed full of a conical shape; others slack, empty or half-empty. A huge parabolic mirror was perched on a crag behind the station, looking like a monstrous, formalized flower. In the whole scene there was only one sign of movement – a small, spacesuited figure prancing madly about on a metal apron in front of the larger dome, waving its arms in a wild welcome.

Duncan left the screen, and went to the cabin. He found Lellie fighting off a large case which, under the influence of deceleration, seemed determined to pin her against the wall. He shoved the case aside, and pulled her out.

'We're there,' he told her. 'Put on your spacesuit.'

Her round eyes ceased to pay attention to the case, and turned towards him. There was no telling from them how she felt, what she thought. She said, simply:

'Thpacethuit. Yith – OK.'

Standing in the airlock of the dome, the outgoing Superintendent paid more attention to Lellie than to the pressure-dial. He knew from experience exactly how long equalizing took, and opened his face-plate without even a glance at the pointer.

'Wish I'd had the sense to bring one,' he observed. 'Could have been mighty useful on the chores, too.'

He opened the inner door, and led through.

'Here it is – and welcome to it,' he said.

The main living room was oddly shaped by reason of the dome's architecture, but it was spacious. It was also exceedingly, sordidly untidy.

'Meant to clean it up – never got around to it, some way,' he added. He looked at Lellie. There was no visible sign of what she thought of the place. 'Never can tell with Marts,' he said uneasily. 'They kind of non-register.'

Duncan agreed: 'I've figured this one looked astonished at being born, and never got over it.'

The other man went on looking at Lellie. His eyes strayed from her to a gallery of pinned-up terrestrial beauties, and back again.

'Sort of funny shape Marts are,' he said, musingly.

'This one's reckoned a good enough looker where she comes from,' Duncan told him, a trifle shortly.

'Sure. No offence, Bud. I guess they'll all seem a funny shape to me after this spell.' He changed the subject. 'I'd better show you the ropes around here.'

Duncan signed to Lellie to open her faceplate so that she could hear him, and then told her to get out of her suit.

The dome was the usual type: double-floored, double-walled, with an insulated and evacuated space between the two; constructed as a unit, and held down by metal bars let into the rock. In the living-quarters there were three more sizeable rooms, able to cope with increased personnel if trade should expand.

'The rest,' the outgoing man explained, 'is the regular station stores, mostly food, air cylinders, spares of one kind and another, and water – you'll need to watch her on water; most women seem to think it grows naturally in pipes.'

Duncan shook his head.

'Not Marts. Living in deserts gives 'em a natural respect for water.'

The other picked up a clip of store-sheets.

'We'll check and sign these later. It's a nice soft job here. Only freight now is rare metalliferous earth. Callisto's not been opened up a lot yet. Handling's easy. They tell you when a crate's on the way: you switch on the radio beacon to bring it in. On dispatch you can't go wrong if you follow the tables.' He looked around the room. 'All home comforts. You read? Plenty of books.' He waved a hand at the packed rows which covered half the inner partition wall. Duncan said he'd never been much of a reader. 'Well, it helps,' said the other. 'Find

75

pretty well anything that's known in that lot. Records there. Fond of music?'

Duncan said he liked a good tune.

'H'm. Better try the other stuff. Tunes get to squirrelling inside your head. Play chess?' He pointed to a board, with men pegged into it. Duncan shook his head.

'Pity. There's a fellow over on Callisto plays a pretty hot game. He'll be disappointed not to finish this one. Still, if I was fixed up the way you are, maybe I'd not have been interested in chess.' His eyes strayed to Lellie again. 'What do you reckon she's going to do here, over and above cooking and amusing you?' he asked.

It was not a question that had occurred to Duncan, but he shrugged.

'Oh, she'll be OK, I guess. There's a natural dumbness about Marts – they'll sit for hours on end, doing damn all. It's a gift they got.'

'Well, it should come in handy here,' said the other.

The regular ship's-call work went on. Cases were unloaded, the metalliferous earths hosed from the bins into the holds. A small ferry-rocket came up from Callisto carrying a couple of time-expired prospectors, and left again with their two replacements. The ship's engineers checked over the station's machinery, made renewals, topped up the water tanks, charged the spent air cylinders, tested, tinkered and tested again before giving their final OK.

Duncan stood outside on the metal apron where not long ago his predecessor had performed his fantastic dance of welcome, to watch the ship take off. She rose straight up, with her jets pushing her gently. The curve of her hull became an elongated crescent shining against the black sky. The main driving jets started to gush white flame edged with pink. Quickly she picked up speed. Before long she had dwindled to a speck which sank behind the ragged skyline.

Quite suddenly Duncan felt as if he, too, had dwindled. He had become a speck upon a barren mass of rock which was itself a speck in the immensity. The indifferent sky about him had no scale. It was an utterly black void wherein his mother-sun and a myriad more suns flared perpetually, without reason or purpose.

The rocks of the satellite itself, rising up in their harsh crests and ridges, were without scale, too. He could not tell which were near or far away; he could not, in the jumble of hard-lit planes and inky shadows, even make out their true form. There was nothing like them to be seen on Earth, or on Mars. Their unweathered edges were sharp as blades: they had been just as sharp as that for millions upon millions of years, and would be for as long as the satellite should last.

The unchanging millions of years seemed to stretch out before and behind him. It was not only himself, it was all life that was a speck, a briefly transitory accident, utterly unimportant to the universe. It was a queer little mote dancing for its chance moment in the light of the eternal suns. Reality was just globes of fire and balls of stone rolling on, senselessly rolling along through emptiness, through time unimaginable, for ever, and ever, and ever . . .

Within his heated suit, Duncan shivered a little. Never before had he been so alone; never so much aware of the vast, callous, futile loneliness of space. Looking out into the blackness, with light that had left a star a million years ago shining into his eyes, he wondered.

'Why?' he asked himself. 'What the heck's it all about, anyway?'

The sound of his own unanswerable question broke up the mood. He shook his head to clear it of speculative nonsense. He turned his back on the universe, reducing it again to its proper status as a background for life in general and human life in particular, and stepped into the airlock.

The job was, as his predecessor had told him, soft. Duncan made his radio contacts wth Callisto at prearranged times. Usually it was little more than a formal check on one another's continued existence, with perhaps an exchange of comment on the radio news. Only occasionally did they announce a dispatch and tell him when to switch on his beacon. Then, in due course, the cylinder-crate would make its appearance, and float slowly down. It was quite a simple matter to couple it up to a bin to transfer the load.

The satellite's day was too short for convenience, and its night, lit by Callisto, and sometimes by Jupiter as well, almost as bright; so they disregarded it, and lived by the calendar-clock which kept Earth time on the Greenwich Meridian setting. At first much of the time had been occupied in disposing of the freight that the ship had left. Some of it into the main dome — necessities for themselves, and other items that would store better where there was warmth and air. Some into the small, airless, unheated dome. The greater part to be stowed and padded carefully into cylinders and launched off to the Callisto base. But once that work had been cleared, the job was certainly soft, too soft . . .

Duncan drew up a programme. At regular intervals he would

inspect this and that, he would waft himself up to the crag and check on the sun-motor there, et cetera. But keeping to an unnecessary programme requires resolution. Sun-motors, for instance, are very necessarily built to run for long spells without attention. The only action one could take if it should stop would be to call on Callisto for a ferry-rocket to come and take them off until a ship should call to repair it. A breakdown there, the Company had explained very clearly, was the only thing that would justify him in leaving his station, with the stores of precious earth, unmanned (and it was also conveyed that to contrive a breakdown for the sake of a change was unlikely to prove worthwhile). One way and another, the programme did not last long.

There were times when Duncan found himself wondering whether the bringing of Lellie had been such a good idea after all. On the purely practical side, he'd not have cooked as well as she did, and probably have pigged it quite as badly as his predecessor had, but if she had not been there, the necessity of looking after himself would have given him some occupation. And even from the angle of company — well, she was that, of a sort, but she was alien, queer; kind of like a half-robot, and dumb at that; certainly no fun. There were, indeed, times — increasingly frequent times, when the very look of her irritated him intensely; so did the way she moved *and* her gestures, *and* her silly pidgin-talk when she talked, *and* her self-contained silence when she didn't, *and* her withdrawnness, *and* all her differentness, *and* the fact that he would have been £2,360 better off without her . . . Nor did she make a serious attempt to remedy her shortcomings, even where she had the means. Her face, for instance. You'd think any girl would try to make her best of that — but did she, hell! There was that left eyebrow again: made her look like a sozzled clown, but a lot she cared . . .

'For heaven's sake,' he told her once more, 'put the cockeyed thing straight. Don't you know how to fix 'em *yet*? And you've got your colour on wrong, too. Look at that picture — now look at yourself in the mirror: a great daub of red all in the wrong place. And your hair, too: getting all like seaweed again. You've got the things to wave it, then for crysake wave it again, and stop looking like a bloody mermaid. I know you can't help being a damn Mart, but you can at least *try* to look like a real woman.'

Lellie looked at the coloured picture, and then compared her reflection with it, critically.

'Yith-OK,' she said, with an equable detachment.

Duncan snorted.

'And that's another thing. Bloody baby-talk! It's not "yith," it's "yes". Y-E-S, yes. So say "yes".'

'Yith,' said Lellie, obligingly.

'Oh for — Can't you *hear* the difference? S-s-s, not th-th-th. Ye-sss.'

'Yith,' she said.

'No. Put your tongue farther back like this—'

The lesson went on for some time. Finally he grew angry.

'Just making a monkey out of me, huh! You'd better be careful, my girl. Now, say "yes".'

She hesitated, looking at his wrathful face.

'Go on, say it.'

'Y-yeth,' she said, nervously.

His hand slapped across her face harder than he had intended. The jolt broke her magnetic contact with the floor, and sent her sailing across the room in a spin of arms and legs. She struck the opposite wall, and rebounded to float helplessly, out of reach of any hold. He strode after her, turned her right way up, and set her on her feet. His left hand clutched her overall in a bunch, just below her throat, his right was raised.

'Again?' he told her.

Her eyes looked helplessly this way and that. He shook her. She tried. At the sixth attempt she managed: 'Yeths.'

He accepted that for the time being.

'You *can* do it, you see — when you try. What you need, my girl, is a bit of firm handling.'

He let her go. She tottered across the room, holding her hands to her bruised face.

A number of times while the weeks drew out so slowly into months Duncan found himself wondering whether he was going to get through. He spun out what work there was as much as he could, but it left still too much time hanging heavy on his hands.

A middle-aged man who has read nothing longer than an occasional magazine article does not take to books. He tired very quickly, as his predecessor had prophesied, of the popular records, and could make nothing of the others. He taught himself the moves in chess from a book, and instructed Lellie in them, intending after a little practice with her to challenge the man on Callisto. Lellie, however, managed to win with such consistency that he had to decide that he had not the right kind of mind for the game. Instead, he taught her a kind of double solitaire, but that didn't last long, either; the cards seemed always to run for Lellie.

Occasionally there was some news and entertainment to be had from the radio, but with Earth somewhere round the other side of the sun just then, Mars screened off half the time by Callisto, and the rotation of the satellite itself, reception was either impossible, or badly broken up.

So mostly he sat and fretted, hating the satellite, angry with himself and irritated by Lellie.

Just the phlegmatic way she went on with her tasks irritated him. It seemed an injustice that she could take it all better than he could simply *because* she was a dumb Mart. When his ill-temper became vocal, the look of her as she listened exasperated him still more.

'For crysake,' he told her one time, 'can't you make that silly face of yours *mean* something? Can't you laugh, or cry, or get mad, or something? It's enough to drive a guy nuts going on looking at a face that's fixed permanent like it was a doll just heard its first dirty story. I know you can't help being dumb, but for heaven's sake crack it up a bit, get some expression into it.'

She went on looking at him without a shadow of a change.

'Go on, you heard me! Smile, damn you, smile!'

Her mouth twitched very slightly.

'Call that a smile! Now, there's a smile!' He pointed to a pin-up with her head split pretty much in half by a smile like a piano keyboard. 'Like that! Like this!' He grinned widely.

'No,' she said. 'My face can't wriggle like Earth faces.'

'Wriggle!' he said, incensed. 'Wriggle, you call it!' He freed himself from the chair's spring-cover, and came towards her. She backed away until she fetched up against the wall. 'I'll make yours wriggle, my girl. Go on, now — smile!' He lifted his hand.

Lellie put her hands up to her face.

'No!' she protested. 'No — no — no!'

It was on the very day that Duncan marked off the eighth completed month that Callisto relayed news of a ship on the way. A couple of days later he was able to make contact with her himself, and confirm her arrival in about a week. He felt as if he had been given several stiff drinks. There were the preparations to make, stores to check, deficiencies to note, a string of nil-nil-nil entries to be made in the log to bring it up to date. He bustled around as he got on with it. He even hummed to himself as he worked, and ceased to be annoyed with Lellie. The effect upon her of the news was imperceptible — but then, what would you expect . . .?

Sharp on her estimated time the ship hung above them, growing slowly larger as her upper jets pressed her down. The moment she was berthed Duncan went aboard, with the feeling that everything in sight was an old friend. The Captain received him warmly, and brought out the drinks. It was all routine — even Duncan's babbling and slightly inebriated manner was the regular thing in the circumstances. The only departure from pattern came when the Captain introduced a man beside him, and explained him.

'We've brought a surprise for you, Superintendent. This is Doctor Whint. He'll be sharing your exile for a bit.'

Duncan shook hands. 'Doctor . . .?' he said, surprisedly.

'Not medicine — science,' Alan Whint told him. 'The Company's pushed me out here to do a geological survey — if geo isn't the wrong word to use. About a year. Hope you don't mind.'

Duncan said conventionally that he'd be glad of the company, and left it at that for the moment. Later, he took him over to the dome. Alan Whint was surprised to find Lellie there; clearly nobody had told him about her. He interrupted Duncan's explanations to say:

'Won't you introduce me to your wife?'

Duncan did so, without grace. He resented the reproving tone in the man's voice; nor did he care for the way he greeted Lellie just as if she were an Earth woman. He was also aware that he had noticed the bruise on her cheek that the colour did not altogether cover. In his mind he classified Alan Whint as one of the smooth, snooty type, and hoped that there was not going to be trouble with him.

It could be, indeed, it was, a matter of opinion who made the trouble when it boiled up some three months later. There had already been several occasions when it had lurked uneasily near. Very likely it would have come into the open long before had Whint's work not taken him out of the dome so much. The moment of touch-off came when Lellie lifted her eyes from the book she was reading to ask:

'What does "female emancipation" mean?'

Alan started to explain. He was only halfway through the first sentence when Duncan broke in:

'Listen — who told you to go putting ideas into her head?'

Alan shrugged his shoulders slightly, and looked at him.

'That's a damn silly question,' he said. 'And, anyway, why shouldn't she have ideas? Why shouldn't anyone?'

'You know what I mean.'

'I never understand you guys who apparently can't *say* what you mean. Try again.'

'All right then. What I mean is this: you come here with your ritzy ways and your snazzy talk, and right from the start you start shoving your nose into things that aren't your business. You begin right off by treating her as if she was some toney dame back home.'

'I hoped so. I'm glad you noticed it.'

'And do you think I didn't see why?'

'I'm quite sure you didn't. You've such a well-grooved mind. You think, in your simple way, that I'm out to get your girl, and you resent that with all the weight of two thousand, three hundred and sixty pounds. But you're wrong: I'm not.'

Duncan was momentarily thrown off his line, then:

'My *wife*,' he corrected. 'She may be only a dumb Mart, but she's legally my wife: and what I say goes.'

'Yes, Lellie is a Mart, as you call it; she may even be your wife, for all I know to the contrary; but dumb, she certainly is not. For one example, look at the speed with which she's learned to read — once someone took the trouble to show her how. I don't think you'd show up any too bright yourself in a language where you only knew a few words, and which you couldn't read.'

'It was none of your business to teach her. She didn't need to read. She was all right the way she was.'

'The voice of the slaver down the ages. Well, if I've done nothing else, I've cracked up your ignorance racket there.'

'And why? — So she'll think you're a great guy. The same reason you talk all toney and smarmy to her. So you'll get her thinking you're a better man than I am.'

'I talk to her the way I'd talk to any woman anywhere — only more simply since she's not had the chance of an education. If she does think I'm a better man, then I agree with her. I'd be sorry if I couldn't.'

'I'll show you who's the better man—' Duncan began.

'You don't need to. I knew when I came here that you'd be a waster, or you'd not be on this job — and it didn't take long for me to find out that you were a goddam bully, too. Do you suppose I've not noticed the bruises? Do you think I've enjoyed having to listen to you bawling out a girl whom you've deliberately kept ignorant and defenceless when she's potentially ten times the sense you have? Having to watch a *clodkopf* like you lording it over your "dumb Mart"? You emetic!'

In the heat of the moment, Duncan could not quite remember what an emetic was, but anywhere else the man would not have got that far before he had waded in to break him up. Yet, even through his anger, twenty years of space experience held — as little more than a boy he had learnt the ludicrous futility of weightless scrapping, and that it was the angry man who always made the bigger fool of himself.

Both of them simmered, but held in. Somehow the occasion was patched up and smoothed over, and for a time things went on much as before.

Alan continued to make his expeditions in the small craft which he had brought with him. He examined and explored other parts of the satellite, returning with specimen pieces of rock which he tested, and arranged, carefully labelled, in cases. In his off times he occupied himself, as before, in teaching Lellie.

That he did it largely for his own occupation as well as from a feeling that it should be done, Duncan did not altogether deny; but he was equally sure that in continued close association one thing leads to another, sooner or later. So far, there had been nothing between them that he could put his finger on — but Alan's term had still some nine months to go, even if he were relieved to time. Lellie was already hero-worshipping. And he was spoiling her more every day by this fool business of treating her as if she were an Earth woman. One day they'd come alive to it — and the next step would be that they would see him as an obstacle that would be better removed. Prevention being better than cure, the sensible course was to see that the situation should never develop. There need not be any fuss about it . . .

There was not.

One day Alan Whint took off on a routine flight to prospect somewhere on the other side of the satellite. He simply never came back. That was all.

There was no telling what Lellie thought about it; but something seemed to happen to her.

For several days she spent almost all her time standing by the main window of the living room, looking out into the blackness at the flaring pinpoints of light. It was not that she was waiting or hoping for Alan's return — she knew as well as Duncan himself that when

83

thirty-six hours had gone by there was no chance of that. She said nothing. Her expression maintained its exasperating look of slight surprise, unchanged. Only in her eyes was there any perceptible difference: they looked a little less live, as if she had withdrawn herself farther behind them.

Duncan could not tell whether she knew or guessed anything. And there seemed to be no way of finding out without planting the idea in her mind — if it were not already there. He was, without admitting it too fully to himself, nervous of her — too nervous to turn on her roundly for the time she spent vacantly mooning out of the window. He had an uncomfortable awareness of how many ways there were for even a dimwit to contrive a fatal accident in such a place. As a precaution he took to fitting new air-bottles to his suit every time he went out, and checking that they were at full pressure. He also took to placing a piece of rock so that the outer door of the air-lock could not close behind him. He made a point of noticing that his food and hers came straight out of the same pot, and watched her closely as she worked. He still could not decide whether she knew, or suspected . . . After they were sure that he was gone, she never once mentioned Alan's name . . .

The mood stayed on her for perhaps a week. Then it changed abruptly. She paid no more attention to the blackness outside. Instead, she began to read, voraciously and indiscriminately.

Duncan found it hard to understand her absorption in the books, nor did he like it, but he decided for the moment not to interfere. It did, at least, have the advantage of keeping her mind off other things.

Gradually he began to feel easier. The crisis was over. Either she had not guessed, or, if she had, she had decided to do nothing about it. Her addiction to books, however, did not abate. In spite of several reminders by Duncan that it was for *company* that he had laid out the not inconsiderable sum of £2,360, she continued, as if determined to work her way through the station's library.

By degrees the affair retreated into the background. When the next ship came Duncan watched her anxiously in case she had been biding her time to hand on her suspicions to the crew. It turned out, however, to be unnecessary. She showed no tendency to refer to the matter, and when the ship pulled out, taking the opportunity with it, he was relievedly able to tell himself that he had really been right all along — she was just a dumb Mart: she had simply forgotten the Alan Whint incident, as a child might.

And yet, as the months of his term ticked steadily away, he found that he had, bit by bit, to revise that estimate of dumbness. She was learning from books things that he did not know himself. It even had some advantages, though it put him in a position he did not care for — when she asked, as she sometimes did now, for explanations, he found it unpleasant to be stumped by a Mart. Having the practical man's suspicion of book-acquired knowledge, he felt it necessary to explain to her how much of the stuff in the book was a lot of nonsense, how they never really came to grips with the problems of life as he had lived it. He cited instances from his own affairs, gave examples from his experience, in fact, he found himself teaching her.

She learnt quickly, too; the practical as well as the book stuff. Of necessity he had to revise his opinions of Marts slightly more — it wasn't that they were altogether dumb as he had thought, just that they were normally too dumb to start using the brains they had. Once started, Lellie was a regular vacuum cleaner for knowledge of all sorts: it didn't seem long before she knew as much about the way-load station as he did himself. Teaching her was not at all what he had intended, but it did provide an occupation much to be preferred to the boredom of the early days. Besides, it had occured to him that she was an appreciating asset . . .

Funny thing, that. He had never before thought of education as anything but a waste of time, but now it seriously began to look as if, when he got her back to Mars, he might recover quite a bit more of the £2,360 than he had expected. Maybe she'd make quite a useful secretary to someone . . . He started to instruct her in elementary book-keeping and finance — in so far as he knew anything about it . . .

The months of service kept on piling up; going a very great deal faster now. During the later stretch, when one had acquired confidence in his ability to get through without cracking up, there was a comfortable feeling about sitting quietly out there with the knowledge of the money gradually piling up at home.

A new find opened up on Callisto, bringing a slight increase in deliveries to the satellite. Otherwise, the routine continued unchanged. The infrequent ships called in, loaded up and went again. And then, surprisingly soon, it was possible for Duncan to say to himself: 'Next ship but one, and I'll be through!' Even more surprisingly soon there came the day when he stood on the metal apron outside the dome, watching a ship lifting herself off on her under-jets and dwindling upwards into the black sky, and was able

85

to tell himself: 'That's the last time I'll see that! When the next ship lifts off this dump, I'll be aboard her, and then — boy, oh boy . . .!'

He stood watching her, one bright spark among the others, until the turn of the satellite carried her below his horizon. Then he turned back to the air-lock — and found the door shut . . .

Once he had decided that there was going to be no repercussion from the Alan Whint affair he had let his habit of wedging it open with a piece of rock lapse. Whenever he emerged to do a job he left it ajar, and it stayed that way until he came back. There was no wind, or anything else on the satellite to move it. He laid hold of the latch-lever irritably, and pushed. It did not move.

Duncan swore at it for sticking. He walked to the edge of the metal apron, and then jetted himself a little round the side of the dome so that he could see in at the window. Lellie was sitting in a chair with the spring-cover fixed across it, apparently lost in thought. The inner door of the air-lock was standing open, so of course the outer could not be moved. As well as the safety-locking device, there was all the dome's air pressure to hold it shut.

Forgetful for the moment, Duncan rapped on the thick glass of the double window to attract her attention; she could not have heard a sound through there, it must have been the movement that caught her eye and caused her to look up. She turned her head, and gazed at him, without moving. Duncan stared back at her. Her hair was still waved, but the eyebrows, the colour, all the other touches that he had insisted upon to make her look as much like an Earth woman as possible, were gone. Her eyes looked back at him, set hard as stones in that fixed expression of mild astonishment.

Sudden comprehension struck Duncan like a physical shock. For some seconds everything seemed to stop.

He tried to pretend to both of them that he had not understood. He made gestures to her to close the inner door of the air-lock. She went on staring back at him, without moving. Then he noticed the book she was holding in her hand, and recognized it. It was not one of the books which the Company had supplied for the station's library. It was a book of verse, bound in blue. It had once belonged to Alan Whint . . .

Panic suddenly jumped out at Duncan. He looked down at the row of small dials across his chest, and then sighed with relief. She had not tampered with his air-supply: there was pressure there enough for thirty hours or so. The sweat that had started out on his brow grew cooler as he regained control of himself. A touch on the jet sent him floating back to the metal apron where he could anchor his magnetic boots, and think it over.

What a bitch! Letting him think all this time that she had forgotten all about it. Nursing it up for him. Letting him work out his time while she planned. Waiting until he was on the very last stretch before she tried her game on. Some minutes passed before his mixed anger and panic settled down and allowed him to think.

Thirty hours! Time to do quite a lot. And even if he did not succeed in getting back into the dome in twenty or so of them, there would still be the last, desperate resort of shooting himself off to Callisto in one of the cylinder-crates.

Even if Lellie were to spill over later about the Whint business what of it? He was sure enough that she did not know *how* it had been done. It would only be the word of a Mart against his own. Very likely they'd put her down as space-crazed.

. . . All the same, some of the mud might stick; it would be better to settle with her here and now — besides, the cylinder idea was risky; only to be considered in the last extremity. There were other ways to be tried first.

Duncan reflected a few minutes longer, then he jetted himself over to the smaller dome. In there, he threw out the switches on the lines which brought power down from the main batteries charged by the sun-motor. He sat down to wait for a bit. The insulated dome would take some time to lose all its heat, but not very long for a drop in the temperature to become perceptible, and visible on the thermometers, once the heat was off. The small capacity, low voltage batteries that were in the place wouldn't be much good to her, even if she did think of lining them up.

He waited an hour, while the faraway sun set, and the arc of Callisto began to show over the horizon. Then he went back to the dome's window to observe results. He arrived just in time to see Lellie fastening herself into her spacesuit by the light of a couple of emergency lamps.

He swore. A simple freezing out process wasn't going to work, then. Not only would the heated suit protect her, but her air supply would last longer than his — and there were plenty of spare bottles in there even if the free air in the dome should freeze solid.

He waited until she had put on the helmet, and then switched on the radio in his own. He saw her pause at the sound of his voice, but she did not reply. Presently she deliberately switched off her receiver. He did not; he kept his open to be ready for the moment when she should come to her senses.

Duncan returned to the apron, and reconsidered. It had been his intention to force his way into the dome without damaging it, if he could. But if she wasn't to be frozen out, that looked difficult. She had the advantage of him in air — and though it was true that in her space-suit she could neither eat nor drink, the same, unfortunately, was true for him. The only way seemed to be to tackle the dome itself.

Reluctantly, he went back to the small dome again, and connected up the electrical cutter. Its cable looped behind him as he jetted across to the main dome once more. Beside the curving metal wall, he paused to think out the job — and the consequences. Once he was through the outer shell there would be a space; then the insulating material — that was OK, it would melt away like butter, and without oxygen it could not catch fire. The more awkward part was going to come with the inner metal skin. It would be wisest to start with a few small cuts to let the air pressure down — and stand clear of it: if it were all to come out with a whoosh he would stand a good chance in his weightless state of being blown a considerable distance by it. And what would she do? Well, she'd very likely try covering up the holes as he made them — a bit awkward if she had the sense to use asbestos packing: it'd have to be the whoosh then . . . Both shells could be welded up again before he re-aerated the place from cylinders . . . The small loss of insulating material wouldn't matter . . . OK, better get down to it, then . . .

He made his connections, and contrived to anchor himself enough to give some purchase. He brought the cutter up, and pressed the trigger-switch. He pressed again, and then swore, remembering that he had shut off the power.

He pulled himself back along the cable, and pushed the switches in again. Light from the dome's windows suddenly illuminated the rocks. He wondered if the restoration of power would let Lellie know what he was doing. What if it did? She'd know soon enough, anyway.

He settled himself down beside the dome once more. This time the cutter worked. It took only a few minutes to slice out a rough, two-foot-circle. He pulled the piece out of the way, and inspected the opening. Then, as he levelled the cutter again, there came a click in his receiver: Lellie's voice spoke in his ear:

'Better not try to break in. I'm ready for that.'

He hesitated, checking himself with his finger on the switch, wondering what counter-move she could have thought up. The threat in her voice made him uneasy. He decided to go round to the window, and see what her game was, if she had one.

She was standing by the table, still dressed in her spacesuit, fiddling with some apparatus she had set up there. For a moment or two he did not grasp the purpose of it.

There was a plastic food-bag, half-inflated, and attached in some way to the table top. She was adjusting a melt plate over it to a small clearance. There was a wire, scotch-taped to the upper side of the bag. Duncan's eye ran back along the wire to a battery, a coil and on to a detonator attached to a bundle of half a dozen blasting-sticks. . .

He was uncomfortably enlightened. It was very simple — ought to be perfectly effective. If the air pressure in the room should fall, the bag would expand; the wire would make contact with the plate: up would go the dome . . .

Lellie finished her adjustment, and connected the second wire to the battery. She turned to look at him through the window. It was infuriatingly difficult to believe that behind that silly surprise frozen on her face she could be properly aware what she was doing.

Duncan tried to speak to her, but she had switched off, and made no attempt to switch on again. She simply stood looking steadily back at him as he blustered and raged. After some minutes she moved across to a chair, fastened the spring-cover across herself and sat waiting.

'All right then,' Duncan shouted inside his helmet. 'But you'll go up with it, damn you!' Which was, of course, nonsense since he had no intention whatever of destroying either the dome or himself.

He had never learnt to tell what went on behind that silly face — she might be coldly determined, or she might not. If it had been a matter of a switch which she must press to destroy the place he might have risked her nerve failing her. But this way, it would be he who operated the switch, just as soon as he should make a hole to let the air out.

Once more he retreated to anchor himself on the apron. There must be *some* way round, some way of getting into the dome without letting the pressure down . . . He thought hard for some minutes, but if there was such a way, he could not find it — besides, there was no guarantee that she'd not set the explosive off herself if she got scared . . .

No — there was no way that he could think of. It would have to be the cylinder-crate to Callisto.

He looked up at Callisto, hanging huge in the sky now, with Jupiter smaller, but brighter, beyond. It wasn't so much the flight, it was the landing there. Perhaps if he were to cram it with all the padding he could find . . . Later on, he could get the Callisto fellows to ferry him back, and they'd find some way to get into the dome, and Lellie would be a mighty sorry girl — *mighty* sorry . . .

Across the levelling there were three cylinders lined up, charged and ready for use. He didn't mind admitting he was scared of that landing: but, scared or not, if she wouldn't even turn on her radio to listen to him, that would be his only chance. And delay would do nothing for him but narrow the margin of his air supply.

He made up his mind, and stepped off the metal apron. A touch on the jets sent him floating across the levelling towards the cylinders. Practice made it an easy thing for him to manoeuvre the nearest one on to the ramp. Another glance at Callisto's inclination helped to reassure him; at least he would reach it all right. If their beacon there was not switched on to bring him in, he ought to be able to call them on the communication radio in his suit when he got closer.

There was not a lot of padding in the cylinder. He fetched more from the others, and packed the stuff in. It was while he paused to figure out a way of triggering the thing off with himself inside, that he realized he was beginning to feel cold. As he turned the knob up a notch, he glanced down at the meter on his chest — in an instant he knew . . . She had known that he would fit fresh air bottles and test them; so it had been the battery, or more likely, the circuit, she had tampered with. The voltage was down to a point where the needle barely kicked. The suit must have been losing heat for some time already.

He knew that he would not be able to last long — perhaps not more than a few minutes. After its first stab, the fear abruptly left him, giving way to an impotent fury. She'd tricked him out of his last chance, but, by God, he could make sure she didn't get away with it. He'd be going, but just one small hole in the dome, and he'd not be going alone . . .

90

The cold was creeping into him, it seemed to come lapping at him icily through the suit. He pressed the jet control and sent himself scudding back towards the dome. The cold was gnawing in at him. His feet and fingers were going first. Only by an immense effort was he able to operate the jet which stopped him by the side of the dome. But it needed one more effort, for he hung there, a yard or so above the ground. The cutter lay where he had left it, a few feet beyond his reach. He struggled desperately to press the control that would let him down to it, but his fingers would no longer move. He wept and gasped at the attempt to make them work, and with the anguish of the cold creeping up his arms. Of a sudden, there was an agonizing, searing pain in his chest. It made him cry out. He gasped — and the unheated air rushed into his lungs, and froze them . . .

In the dome's living room Lellie stood waiting. She had seen the spacesuited figure come sweeping across the levelling at an abnormal speed. She understood what it meant. Her explosive device was already disconnected; now she stood alert, with a thick rubber mat in her hand, ready to clap it over any hole that might appear. She waited one minute, two minutes . . . When five minutes had passed she went to the window. By putting her face close to the pane and looking sideways she was able to see the whole of one spacesuited leg and part of another. They hung there horizontally, a few feet off the ground. She watched them for several minutes. Their gradual downward drift was barely perceptible.

She left the window, and pushed the mat out of her hand so that it floated away across the room. For a moment or two she stood thinking. Then she went to the bookshelves and pulled out the last volume of the encyclopaedia. She turned the pages, and satisfied herself on the exact status and claims which are connoted by the word 'widow'.

She found a pad of paper and a pencil. For a minute she hesitated, trying to remember the method she had been taught, then she started to write down figures, and became absorbed in them. At last she lifted her head, and contemplated the result: £5,000 per annum for five years, at 6 per cent compound interest, worked out at a nice little sum — quite a small fortune for a Martian.

But then she hesitated again. Very likely a face that was not set for ever in a mould of slightly surprised innocence would have frowned a little at that point, because, of course, there was a deduction that had to be made — a matter of £2,360.

John Wyndham

Patrick O'Brian

Patrick O'Brian is perhaps best known for his series of naval novels set in the eighteenth century. There are twelve in the collection to date, including *HMS Surprise*. He also writes short stories and has translated the works of Simone de Beauvoir and other writers from French into English.

Samphire

Sheer, sheer, the white cliff rising, straight up from the sea, so far that the riding waves were nothing but ripples on a huge calm. Up there, unless you leaned over, you did not see them break, but for all the distance the thunder of the water came loud. The wind, too, tearing in from the sea, rushing from a clear, high sky, brought the salt tang of the spray on their lips.

They were two, standing up there on the very edge of the cliff: they had left the levelled path and come down to the break itself and the man was crouched, leaning over as far as he dared.

'It *is* a clump of samphire, Molly,' he said; then louder, half turning, 'Molly, it *is* samphire. I *said* it was samphire, didn't I?' He had a high, rather unmasculine voice, and he emphasized his words.

His wife did not reply, although she had heard him the first time. The round of her chin was trembling like a child's before it cries: there was something in her throat so strong that she could not have spoken it if it had been for her life.

She stepped a little closer, feeling cautiously for a firm foothold, and she was right on him and she caught the smell of his hairy tweed jacket. He straightened so suddenly that he brushed against her. 'Hey, look out,' he said, 'I almost trod on your foot. Yes, it *was* samphire. I said so as soon as I saw it from down there. Have a look.'

She could not answer, so she knelt and crawled to the edge. Heights terrified her, always had. She could not close her eyes; that only made it worse. She stared unseeing, while the brilliant air and the sea and the noise of the sea assaulted her terrified mind and she clung insanely to the thin grass. Three times he pointed it out, and the third time she heard him so as to be able to understand his words. '. . . fleshy leaves. You see the fleshy leaves? They used them for pickles. Samphire pickles!' He laughed, excited by the wind, and put his hand on her shoulder. Even then she writhed away, covering it by getting up and returning to the path.

He followed her. 'You noted the *fleshy leaves*, didn't you, Molly? They allow the plant to store its nourishment. Like a cactus. Our *native cactus*. I *said* it was samphire at once, didn't I, although I have never actually seen it before. We could almost get it with a stick.'

He was pleased with her for having looked over, and said that she was coming along very well: she remembered — didn't she? — how he had had to persuade her and persuade her to come up even the smallest cliff at first, how he had even to be a little firm. And now there she was going up the highest of them all, as bold as brass; and it was quite a dangerous cliff too, he said, with a keen glance out to sea, jutting his chin; but there she was as bold as brass looking over the top of it. He had been quite right insisting, hadn't he? It was worth it when you were there, wasn't it? Between these questions he waited for a reply, a 'yes' or hum of agreement. If he had not insisted she would always have stayed down there on the beach, wouldn't she? Like a lazy puss. He said, wagging his finger to show that he was not quite in earnest, that she should always listen to her Lacey (this was a pet name that he had coined for himself). Lacey was her lord and master, wasn't he? Love, honour, and obey?

He put his arm round her when they came to a sheltered turn of the path and began to fondle her, whispering in his secret night-voice, Tss-tss-tss, but he dropped her at once when some coast-guards appeared.

As they passed he said, 'Good day, men,' and wanted to stop to ask them what they were doing but they walked quickly on.

★   ★   ★

In the morning she said she would like to see the samphire again. He was very pleased and told the hotel-keeper that she was becoming quite the little botanist. He had already told him and the nice couple from Letchworth (they were called Jones and had a greedy daughter: he was an influential solicitor, and Molly would be a clever girl to be nice to them), he had already told them about the samphire, and he had said how he had recognized it at once from lower down, where the path turned, although he had only seen specimens in a *hortus siccus* and illustrations in books.

On the way he stopped at the tobacconist on the promenade to buy a stick. He was in high spirits. He told the man at once that he did not smoke, and made a joke about the shop being a house of ill-*fume*; but the tobacconist did not understand. He looked at the sticks that were in the shop but he did not find one for his money and they went out. At the next tobacconist, by the pier, he made the same joke to the man there. She stood near the door, not looking at anything. In the end he paid the marked price for an ash walking stick with a crook, though at first he had proposed a shilling less: he told the man that they were not ordinary summer people, because they were going to have a villa there.

Walking along past the pier towards the cliff path, he put the stick on his shoulder with a comical gesture, and when they came to the car park where a great many people were coming down to the beach with picnics and pneumatic rubber toys he sang, 'We are the boys that nothing can tire; we are the boys that gather samphire.' When a man who was staying in the same hotel passed near them, he called out that they were going to see if they could get a bunch of jolly good samphire that they had seen on the cliff yesterday. The man nodded.

It was a long way to the highest cliff, and he fell silent for a little while. When they began to climb he said that he would never go out without a stick again; it was a fine, honest thing, an ashplant, and a great help. Didn't she think it was a great help? Had she noticed how he had chosen the best one in the shop, and really it was very cheap, though perhaps they had better go without tea tomorrow to make it up. She remembered, didn't she, what they had agreed after their discussion about an exact allowance for every day? He was walking a few feet ahead of her, so that each time he had to turn his head for her answer.

It was blowing harder than the day before on the top, and for the last hundred yards he kept silent, or at least she did not hear him say anything.

At the turn of the path he cried, 'It is still there. Oh jolly good. It is still there, Molly,' and he pointed out how he had first seen the samphire, and repeated, shouting over the wind, that he had been sure of it at once.

For a moment she looked at him curiously while he stared over and up where the plant grew on the face of the cliff, the wind ruffling the thin, fluffy hair that covered his baldness, and a keen expression on his face; and for a moment she wondered whether it was perhaps possible that he saw beauty there. But the moment was past and the voice took up again its unceasing dumb cry: Go on, oh, go on, for Christ's sake, go on, go on, go on, oh go *on*.

They were there. He had made her look over. 'Note the fleshy leaves,' he had said; and he had said something about samphire pickle! and how the people at the hotel would stare when they brought it back. That was just before he began to crouch over, turned from her so that his voice was lost.

He was leaning right over. It was quite true when he said that he had no fear of heights: once he had astonished the workmen on the steeple of her uncle's church by walking among the scaffolding and planks with all the aplomb of a steeplejack. He was reaching down with his left arm, his right leg doubled under him and his right arm extended on the grass: his other leg was stretched out along the break of the cliff.

★　　★　　★

Once again there was the strong grip in her throat; her stomach was rigid and she could not keep her lip from trembling. She could hardly see, but as he began to get up her eyes focused. She was already there, close on him — she had never gone back to the path this time. God give me strength, but as she pushed him she felt her arms weak like jelly.

Instantly his face turned; absurd, baby-face surprise and a shout unworded. The extreme of horror on it, too. He had been half up when she thrust at him, with his knee off the ground, the stick hand over and the other clear of the grass. He rose, swaying out. For a second the wind bore his body and the stick scrabbled furiously for a purchase on the cliff. There where the samphire grew, a little above; it found a hard ledge, gripped. Motionless in equilibrium for one timeless space — a cinema stopped in action — then his right hand gripped the soil, tore, ripped the grass and he was up, from the edge, crouched, gasping huge sobbing draughts of air on the path.

He was screaming at her in an agonized falsetto interrupted by painful gasps, searching for air and life. 'You pushed me, Molly you — pushed me. You — pushed me.'

She stood silent, looking down and the voice rushed over her. You pushed — you pushed me — Molly. She found she could swallow again, and the hammering in her throat was less. By now his voice had dropped an octave: he had been speaking without a pause but for his gasping — the gasping had stopped now, and he was sitting there normally '. . . not well; a spasm. Wasn't it, Molly?' he was saying; and she heard him say 'accident' sometimes.

Still she stood, stone-still and grey and later he was saying '. . . *possibly* live together? How can we *possibly* look at one another? After this?' And some time after it seemed to her that he had been saying something about their having taken their room for the month . . . accident was the word, and spasm, and not well — fainting? It was, wasn't it, Molly? There was an unheard note in his voice.

She turned and began to walk down the path. He followed at once. By her side he was, and his face was turned to hers, peering into her face, closed face. His visage, his whole face, everything, had fallen to pieces: she looked at it momentarily — a very old terribly frightened comforting-itself small child. He had fallen off a cliff all right.

He touched her arm, still speaking, pleading, 'It *was* that, wasn't it, Molly? You didn't push me, Molly. It was an accident. . .'

She turned her dying face to the ground, and there were her feet marching on the path; one, the other; one, the other; down, down, down.

Patrick O'Brian

Jan Mark

Jan Mark was born and brought up in Welwyn Garden City, although her family originates from London. She was educated at Ashford Grammar School and then at Canterbury College of Art. She began writing at a very early age and at fifteen won second prize in a *Daily Mirror* short story competition. Later, while teaching art in Gravesend, she started to write comic plays.

Jan Mark has since written many short stories, novels and plays for young people and has won many awards for her books, including the *Carnegie Medal* in 1976 for *Thunder and Lightnings*, and in 1983 for *Handles*. Her first adult novel, *Zeno Was Here*, was published in 1987 to good reviews; it was subsequently published in the USA in the spring of 1988.

Her stories and novels have been translated into eight different languages and in 1986, Thames Television bought the film rights for *Trouble Halfway* and *Frankie's Hat*.

Jan Mark is married with two children. She lives in Oxford, where she is Arts Council Writer/Fellow in Residence at Oxford Polytechnic.

Feet

Unlike the Centre Court at Wimbledon, the Centre Court at our school is the one nobody wants to play on. It is made of asphalt and has dents in it, like Ryvita. All the other courts are grass, out in the sun; Centre Court is in between the science block and the canteen and when there is a Governors' Meeting the governors use it as a car park. The sun only shines on Centre Court at noon in June and there is green algae growing round the edges. When I volunteered to be an umpire at the annual tennis tournament I might have known that I was going to end up on Centre Court.

'You'd better go on Centre Court,' said Mr Evans, 'as it's your first time. It won't matter so much if you make mistakes.' I love Mr Evans. He is so tactful and he looks like an orang-utan in his track suit. I believe myself that he swings from the pipes in the changing room, but I haven't personally observed this, you understand. He just looks as if he might enjoy swinging from things. He has very long arms. Probably he can peel bananas with his toes, which have little tufts of hair on, like beard transplants. I saw them once.

So I was sitting up in my umpire's chair, just like Wimbledon, with an official school pencil and a pad of score cards and I wasn't making any mistakes. This was mainly because they were all first round matches, the six love, six love kind, to get rid of the worst players. All my matches were ladies' doubles which is what you call the fifth and sixth year girls when they are playing tennis although not at any other time. We didn't get any spectators except some first year boys who came to look at the legs and things and Mr Evans, on and off, who was probably there for the same reason.

All the men's matches were on the grass courts, naturally, so I didn't see what I wanted to see which was Michael Collier. I suppose it was the thought of umpiring Collier that made me put my name down in the first place, before I remembered about ending up on Centre

Court. I could only hope that I would be finished in time for the Men's Final so that I could go and watch it because Collier would definitely be in the final. People said that it was hardly worth his while playing, really, why didn't they just give him the trophy and have done with it?

Looking back, I dare say that's what he thought, too.

So anyway, I got rid of all my ladies' doubles and sat around waiting for a mixed doubles. It was cold and windy on Centre Court since it wasn't noon in June, and I wished I had worn a sweater instead of trying to look attractive sort of in short sleeves. Sort of is right. That kind of thing doesn't fool anyone. I had these sandals too which let the draught in something rotten. I should have worn wellies. No one would have noticed. Nobody looks at feet.

After the mixed doubles which was a fiasco I thought of going in to get a hot drink — tea or coffee or just boiling water would have done — when I noticed this thing coming down the tramlines and trying to walk on one leg like Richard the Third only all in white.

Richard the Bride.

It was using a tennis racquet head down as a walking stick which is not done, like cheating at cards. No gentleman would do this to his tennis racquet. This is no gentleman.

'Ho,' says this Richard the Third person. 'Me Carson. You Jane.'

This does not quite qualify as Pun of the Week because he *is* Carson and I *am* Jane. He is Alan Carson from the sixth form — only he is at Oxford now — and he would not know me from Adam only he is a neighbour and used to baby-sit with me once. This is humiliating and I don't tell people.

Carson is known to do a number of strange things and walking on one leg may be one of them for all I know so I do not remark on it.

'Hello, Carson,' I said, very coolly. I was past sounding warm, anyway. 'Where are you going?'

Carson sits down on a stacking chair at the foot of my ladder.

'I'm going to get changed,' he says.

'Did you lose your match?' I say, tactfully like Mr Evans. (I am surprised because he is next most likely after Collier to be in the final.)

'No, I won,' says Carson. 'But it was a Pyrrhic victory,' and he starts whanging the net post with his tennis racquet, *boing boing*. (This is not good for it either, I should think.)

I have heard about Pyrrhic victories but I do not know what they are.

'What's a Pyrrhic victory?' I said.

'One you can do without,' said Carson. 'Named after King Pyrrhus of Epirus who remarked, after beating the Romans in a battle, "One more win like this and we've had it", on account of the Romans badly chewing up his army.'

'Oh,' I said. 'And did he get another win?'

'Yes,' said Carson. 'But then he got done over at the battle of Beneventum by Curius Dentatus the famous Roman general with funny teeth. Now I just knocked spots off Pete Baldwin in the quarter-final and I'm running up to the net to thank him for a jolly good game old boy, when I turn my ankle and fall flat on my back. It's a good thing,' he added, thoughtfully, 'that I didn't get as far as the net, because I should have jumped over it and *then* fallen flat on my back.'

I could see his point. That's the kind of thing that happens to me.

'I should have met Mick Collier in the semifinal,' said Carson. 'Now he'll have a walkover. Which should suit him. He doesn't care where he puts his feet.'

'Who will he play in the final?' I say, terribly pleased for Collier as well as being sorry for Carson whose ankle is definitely swelling as even I can see without my glasses which I do not wear in between matches although everyone can see I wear them because of the red mark across my nose.

'Mills or McGarrity,' says Carson. 'Mills is currently beating McGarrity and then Collier will beat Mills — to pulp — and no one will be surprised. I don't know why we bother,' he says, tiredly, 'it was a foregone conclusion.' And he limps away, dragging his injured foot and not even trying to be funny about it because obviously it hurts like hell.

Then it started to rain.

Everybody came and sheltered in the canteen and griped, especially Mills and McGarrity, especially Mills who was within an inch of winning and wanted to get that over and have a crack at Collier who was a more worthy opponent. McGarrity heard all this and looked as if he would like to give Mills a dead leg — or possibly a dead head.

Then it stops raining and Mr Evans the games master and Miss Sylvia Truman who is our lady games master go out and skid about on the grass courts to see if they are safe. They are not. Even then I do not realize what is going to happen because Collier comes over to the dark corner where I am skulking with my cold spotty arms and starts talking to *me*!

'Jane Turner, isn't it?' he says. He must have asked somebody because he couldn't possibly know otherwise. I was only a fourth year then.

And I say, Yes.

And he says, 'I see you every day on the bus, don't I?'

And I say Yes although I travel downstairs and he travels up, among the smokers although of course he doesn't smoke himself because of his athlete's lungs.

And he says, 'You're an umpire today, aren't you?'

And I say Yes.

And he says, 'Do you play?'

And I say Yes which I do and not badly but I don't go in for tournaments because people watch and if I was being watched I would foul it up.

'We have a court at home,' he says which I know because he is a near neighbour like Carson although me and Carson live on the Glebelands Estate and the Colliers live in the Old Rectory. And then he says, *'You ought to come over and play, sometime.'*

And I can't believe this but I say Yes. Yes please. Yes, I'd like that. And I still don't believe it.

And he says, 'Bring your cousin and make up a foursome. That was your cousin who was sitting next to you, wasn't it, on the bus?' and I know he must have been asking about me because my cousin Dawn is only staying with us for a week.

And I say Yes, and he says, 'Come on Friday, then,' and I say Yes. Again. And I wonder how I can last out till Friday evening. It is only three-fifteen on Wednesday.

And then Mr Evans and Miss Sylvia Truman come in from skidding about and Mr Evans, finalist in the All-England Anthropoid Ape Championships says, 'The grass is kaput. We'll have to finish up on Centre Court. Come on Collier. Come on Mills,' and McGarrity says, 'Mills hasn't beaten me yet, Sir,' and Sir says, 'Oh, well,' and doesn't say, 'It's a foregone conclusion,' and Miss Sylvia Truman says, 'Well hurry up and finish him off, Mills,' in a voice that McGarrity isn't supposed to hear but does.

(If Miss Sylvia Truman *was* a man instead of just looking like one, McGarrity would take her apart, but doesn't, because she isn't. Also, she is much bigger than McGarrity.)

And Sir says, 'Where's the umpire?' and I say I am and Sir says, 'Can you manage?' and I say, 'I haven't made any mistakes yet.'

'But it's the *final*,' says Fiery Fred Truman who thinks I am an imbecile — I have heard her — but I say I can manage and I am desperate to do it because of Collier playing and perhaps Sir has been fortifying himself with the flat bottle he thinks we don't know about but which we can see the outline of in his hip pocket, because he says, 'All right, Jane,' and I can't believe it.

But anyway, we all go out to the damp green canyon that is Centre Court and I go up my ladder and Mills finishes off McGarrity love-love-love-love and still I don't make any mistakes.

And then suddenly *everybody* is there to watch because it is Mills versus Collier and we all want Collier to win.

Collier comes and takes off his sweater and hangs it on the rung of my chair and says, 'Don't be too hard on me, Jane,' with that smile that would make you love him even if you didn't like him, and I say, 'I've got to be impartial,' and he smiles and I wish that I didn't have to be impartial and I am afraid that I won't be impartial.

He says, 'I won't hold it against you, Jane.' And he says, 'Don't forget Friday.'

I say, 'I won't forget Friday,' as loudly as I can so that as many people as possible will hear, which they do.

You can see them being surprised all round the court.

'And don't forget your cousin,' he says, and I say, 'Oh, she's going home on Thursday morning.'

'Some other time, then,' he says.

'No, no,' I said. '*I* can come on Friday,' but he was already walking onto the court and he just looked over his shoulder and said, 'No, it doesn't matter,' and all round the court you could see people not being surprised. And I was there on that lousy stinking bloody ladder and *everybody* could see me.

I thought I was going to cry and spent a long time putting my glasses on. Collier and Mills began to knock up and I got out the pencil and the score cards and broke the point off the pencil. I didn't have another one and I didn't want to show my face asking anybody to lend me one so I had to bite the wood away from the lead and of course it didn't have a proper point and made two lines instead of one. And gritty.

And then I remembered that I had to start them off so I said 'Play, please. Collier to serve.' He had won the toss. Naturally.

My voice had gone woolly and my glasses had steamed over and I was sure people were laughing, even if they weren't. Then I heard this voice down by my feet saying, 'Let him get on with it. If he won't play with you on Friday he can play with himself,' which kind of remark would normally make me go red only I was red already. I looked down and there was Carson looking not at all well because of his foot, probably, but he gave me an evil wink and I remembered that he was a very kind person, really. I remembered that he sometimes gave me a glass of beer when he was baby-sitting. (I was only eleven, then, when he baby-sat. My mother was fussy about leaving us and there was my baby brother as well. He wasn't really sitting with *me*.)

So I smiled and he said, 'Watch the court, for God's sake, they've started,' and they had.

'That's a point to Collier,' he said, and I marked it down and dared not take my eyes off court after that, even to thank him. I looked down again when they changed ends and Carson had gone. (I asked him later where he had gone to and he said he went to throw up. I hope all this doesn't make Carson sound too *coarse*. He was in great pain. It turned out that he had broken a bone in his foot but we didn't know that, then. There are a lot of bones in the foot although you think of it as being solid — down to the toes, at any rate.)

Collier wasn't having it all his own way hooray hooray. Mills was very good too and the first set went to a tiebreak. I still wasn't making any mistakes. But when they came off the court after the tiebreak which Collier won, and did Wimbledonly things with towels and a bit of swigging and spitting, he kept not looking at me. I mean, you could definitely see him *not* looking at me. Everybody could see him *not* looking at me; remembering what he had said about Friday and what I had said about Friday, as loudly as I could.

I was nearly crying again, and what with that and the state of the official school pencil, the score card began to be in a bit of a mess and I suddenly realized that I was putting Collier's points on the wrong line. And of course, I called out 'Advantage Mills,' when it should have been forty-thirty to Collier and he yelled at me to look at what I was doing.

You don't argue with the umpire. You certainly don't *yell* at the umpire, but he did. I know I was wrong but he didn't have to yell. I kept thinking about him yelling and about Friday and in the next game I made the same mistake again and he was saying 'That's all I need, a cross-eyed umpire; there's eight hundred people in this school; can't we find *one* with 20-20 vision?' If Fiery Fred or Orang-Evans had been listening he might not have said it, but he was up by the net and facing away from them. He got worse and worse. Abusive.

Then Mills won the next game without any help from me and I thought, At least he's not having another walkover, and I remembered what Carson had said. 'He doesn't care where he puts his feet.' And of course, after that, I couldn't help looking at his feet and Carson was right. He didn't care where he put them. He had this very fantastic service that went up about ten yards before he hit the ball, but his toes were over the base line three times out of five. I don't know why nobody noticed. I suppose they were all watching the fantastic ten yard service and anyway, nobody looks at feet.

At first I forgot that this was anything to do with me; when I did remember I couldn't bear to do anything about it, at first. Then it was Mills who was serving and I had time to think.

I thought, Why should he get away with it?

Then I thought, He gets away with everything, and I realized that Carson probably hadn't been talking about real feet but feet was all I could think of.

Collier served. His feet were not where they should have been.

'Fifteen — love.'

I thought, I'll give you one more chance, because he was playing so well and I didn't want to spoil that fantastic service. But he had his chance, and he did it again. It was a beautiful shot, an ace, right down the centre line, and Mills never got near it.

I said. 'Foot fault.'

There was a sort of mumbling noise from everyone watching and Collier scowled but he had to play the second service. Mills tipped it back over the net and Collier never got near it.

'Fifteen all.'

'Foot fault.'

He was going to argue but of course he couldn't because feet is not what he looked at when he was serving.

'Fifteen — thirty.' His second service wasn't very good, really.

'Foot fault.'

'Fifteen — forty.'

And then he did begin to look, and watching his feet he had to stop watching the ball and all sorts of things began to happen to his service.

Mills won that set.

'What the hell are you playing at, Turner?' said Collier, when they came off court and he called me a vindictive little cow while he was towelling and spitting but honestly, I never called foot fault if it wasn't.

They went back for the third set and it was Collier's service. He glared at me like he had deathray eyeballs and tossed up the first ball. And looked up.

And looked down at his feet.

And looked up again, but it was too late and the ball came straight down and bounced and rolled away into the crowd.

So he served again, looked up, looked down, and tried to move back and trod on his own foot and fell over.

People laughed. A laugh sounds terrible on Centre Court with all those walls to bounce off. Some of the algae had transferred itself to his shorts.

By now, *everybody* was looking at his feet.

He served a double fault.

'So who's winning?' said Alan Carson, back again and now looking greener than Collier's shorts. I knew he would understand because he *had* come back instead of going home to pass out which was what he should have been doing.

'I am,' I said, miserably.

'Two Pyrrhic victories in one afternoon?' said Alan. 'That must be some kind of record.'

'It must be,' I said. 'It's got a hole in it.'

Jan Mark

Doris Lessing

Doris Lessing was born in Khermanshah, Persia (now Iran) in 1919, of British parents. When she was five the family moved to a farm in Southern Rhodesia (now Zimbabwe). She left school at fifteen and worked as a nursemaid and then as a shorthand typist and a telephone operator in Salisbury.

Before leaving Africa for England in 1949, she had married twice and had become involved in radical politics. She took her youngest child with her and the manuscript for her first novel, *The Grass is Singing*, which was published in 1950. This was followed by five novels collectively entitled, *Children of Violence*, published between 1952 and 1969. Her writing was well-received and she went on to write further novels, short stories and non-fiction. He best known book is perhaps *The Golden Notebook*, published in 1962, which is seen as a great landmark by the Women's Movement.

Her concern for politics, the changing role of women and her awareness of the possibility of catastrophe are all issues reflected in her writing.

Doris Lessing's most recent work includes a collection of novels, *Canopus in Argos: Archives*, which have been described as 'space fiction', and her latest book, the disturbing story of *The Fifth Child*.

A Woman on a Roof

It was during the week of hot sun, that June.

Three men were at work on the roof, where the leads got so hot, they had the idea of throwing water on to cool them. But the water steamed, then sizzled; and they made jokes about getting an egg from some woman in the flats under them, to poach it for their dinner. By two it was not possible to touch the guttering they were replacing, and they speculated about what workmen did in regularly hot countries. Perhaps they should borrow kitchen gloves with the egg? They were all a bit dizzy, not used to the heat; and they shed their coats and stood side by side squeezing themselves into a foot wide patch of shade against a chimney, careful to keep their feet in the thick socks and boots out of the sun. There was a fine view across several acres of roofs. Not far off a man sat in a deck chair reading the newspapers. Then they saw her, between chimneys, about fifty yards away. She lay face down on a brown blanket. They could see the top part of her: black hair, a flushed solid back, arms spread out.

'She's stark naked,' said Stanley, sounding annoyed.

Harry, the oldest, a man of about forty-five, said: 'Looks like it.'

Young Tom, seventeen, said nothing, but he was excited and grinning.

Stanley said: 'Someone'll report her if she doesn't watch out.'

'She thinks no one can see,' said Tom, craning his head all ways, to see more.

At this point the woman, still lying prone, brought her two hands up behind her shoulders with the ends of a scarf in them, tied it behind her back, and sat up. She wore a red scarf tied around her breasts and brief red bikini pants. This being the first day of the sun she was white, flushing red. She sat smoking, and did not look up when Stanley let out a wolf whistle. Harry said: 'Small things amuse small minds,' leading the way back to their part of the roof, but it was scorching. Harry said: 'Wait, I'm going to rig up some shade,' and disappeared down the skylight into the building. Now that he'd gone, Stanley and Tom went to the farthest point they could to peer at the woman. She had moved, and all they would see were two pink legs stretched on the blanket. They whistled and shouted but the legs did not move. Harry came back with a blanket and shouted: 'Come on, then.' He sounded irritated with them. They clambered back to him and he said to Stanley: 'What about your missus?' Stanley was newly married, about three months. Stanley said, jeering: 'What about my missus?' – preserving his independence. Tom said nothing, but his mind was full of the nearly naked woman. Harry slung the blanket, which he had borrowed from a friendly woman downstairs, from the stem of a television aerial to a row of chimney pots. This shade fell across the piece of gutter they had to replace. But the shade kept moving, they had to adjust the blanket, and not much progress was made. At last some of the heat left the roof, and they worked fast, making up for lost time. First Stanley, then Tom, made a trip to the end of the roof to see the woman. 'She's on her back,' Stanley said, adding a jest which made Tom snicker, and the older man smile tolerantly. Tom's report was that she hadn't moved, but it was a lie. He wanted to keep what he had seen to himself: he had caught her in the act of rolling down the little red pants over her hips till they were no more than a small triangle. She was on her back, fully visible, glistening with oil.

Next morning, as soon as they came up, they went to look. She was already there, face down, arms spread out, naked except for the little red pants. She had turned brown in the night. Yesterday she was a scarlet and white woman, today she was a brown woman. Stanley let out a whistle. She lifted her head, startled, as if she'd been asleep, and looked straight over at them. The sun was in her eyes, she blinked and stared, then she dropped her head again. At this gesture of indifference, they all three, Stanley, Tom and old Harry, let out whistles and yells. Harry was doing it in parody of the younger men, making fun of them, but he was also angry. They were all angry because of her utter indifference to the three men watching her.

'Bitch,' said Stanley.

'She should ask us over,' said Tom, snickering.

Harry recovered himself and reminded Stanley: 'If she's married, her old man wouldn't like that.'

'Christ,' said Stanley virtuously, 'if my wife lay about like that, for everyone to see, I'd soon stop her.'

Harry said, smiling: 'How do you know, perhaps she's sunning herself at this very moment?'

'Not a chance, not on our roof.' The safety of his wife put Stanley into a good humour, and they went to work. But today it was hotter than yesterday; and several times one or the other suggested they should tell Matthew, the foreman, and ask to leave the roof until the heat wave was over. But they didn't. There was work to be done in the basement of the big block of flats, but up here they felt free, on a different level from ordinary humanity shut in the streets or the buildings. A lot more people came out on to the roofs that day, for an hour at midday. Some married couples sat side by side in deck chairs, the women's legs stockingless and scarlet, the men in vests with reddening shoulders.

The woman stayed on her blanket, turning herself over and over. She ignored them, no matter what they did. When Harry went off to fetch more screws, Stanley said: 'Come on.' Her roof belonged to a different system of roofs, separated from theirs at one point by about twenty feet. It meant a scrambling climb from one level to another, edging along parapets, clinging to chimneys, while their big boots slipped and slithered, but at last they stood on a small square projecting roof looking straight down at her, close. She sat smoking, reading a book. Tom thought she looked like a poster, or a magazine cover, with the blue sky behind her and her legs stretched out. Behind her a great crane at work on a new building in Oxford Street swung its black arm across the roofs in a great arc. Tom imagined himself at work on the crane, adjusting the arm to swing over and pick her up and swing her back across the sky to drop her near him.

They whistled. She looked up at them, cool and remote, then went on reading. Again, they were furious. Or rather, Stanley was. His sun-heated face was screwed into rage as he whistled again and again, trying to make her look up. Young Tom stopped whistling. He stood beside Stanley excited, grinning; but he felt as if he were saying to the woman: 'Don't associate me with *him*,' for his grin was apologetic. Last night he had thought of the unknown woman before he slept, and she had been tender with him. This tenderness he was remembering as he shifted his feet by the jeering, whistling Stanley, and watched the indifferent, healthy brown woman a few feet off, with the gap that plunged to the street between them. Tom thought it was romantic, it was like being high on two hill tops. But there was a shout from Harry, and they clambered back. Stanley's face was hard, really angry. The boy kept looking at him and wondered why he hated the woman so much, for already he loved her.

They played their little games with the blanket, trying to trap shade to work under; but again it was not until nearly four that they could work seriously, and they were exhausted, all three of them. They were grumbling about the weather, by now. Stanley was in a thoroughly bad humour. When they made their routine trip to see the woman before they packed up for the day, she was apparently asleep, face down, her back all naked save for the scarlet triangle on her buttocks. 'I've got a good mind to report her to the police,' said Stanley, and Harry said: 'What's eating you? What harm's she doing?'

'I tell you, if she was my wife!'

'But she isn't, is she?' Tom knew that Harry, like himself, was uneasy at Stanley's reaction. He was normally a sharp young man, quick at his work, making a lot of jokes, good company.

'Perhaps it will be cooler tomorrow?' said Harry.

But it wasn't, it was hotter, if anything, and the weather forecast said the good weather would last. As soon as they were on the roof, Harry went over to see if the woman were there, and Tom knew it was to prevent Stanley going, to put off his bad humour. Harry had grown-up children, a boy the same age as Tom, and the youth trusted and looked up to him.

Harry came back and said: 'She's not there.'

'I bet her old man has put his foot down,' said Stanley, and Harry and Tom caught each other's eyes and smiled behind the young married man's back.

Harry suggested they should get permission to work in the basement, and they did, that day. But before packing up Stanley said: 'Let's have a breath of fresh air.' Again Harry and Tom smiled at each other as they followed Stanley up to the roof, Tom in the devout conviction that he was there to protect the woman from Stanley. It was about five-thirty, and a calm full sunlight lay over the roofs. The great crane still swung its black arm from Oxford Street to above their heads. She was not there. Then there was a flutter of white from behind a parapet, and she stood up, in a belted white dressing gown. She had been there all day, probably, but on a different patch of roof, to hide from them. Stanley did not whistle, he said nothing, but watched the woman bend to collect papers, books, cigarettes, then fold the blanket over her arm. Tom was thinking: If they weren't here, if they weren't here, I'd go over and say . . . what? But he knew from his nightly dreams of her that she was kind and friendly. Perhaps she would ask him down in to her flat? Perhaps . . . he stood watching her disappear down the skylight. As she went, Stanley let out a shrill derisive yell, she started, and it seemed as if she nearly fell. She clutched to save herself, they could hear things falling. She looked straight at them, angry. Harry said, facetiously: 'Better be careful on those slippery ladders, love.' Tom knew he said it to save her from Stanley, but she could not know it. She vanished, frowning. Tom was full of a secret delight, because he knew her anger was for the others, not for him.

'Roll on some rain,' said Stanley, bitter, looking at the blue evening sky.

Next day was cloudless, and they decided to finish the work in the basement. They felt excluded, shut in the grey cement basement fitting pipes, from the holiday atmosphere of London in a heat wave. At lunchtime they came up for some air, but while the married couples, and the men in shirtsleeves or vests, were there, she was not there, either on her usual patch of roof or where she had been yesterday. They all, even Harry, clambered about, between chimney-pots, over parapets, the hot leads stinging their fingers. There was not a sign of her. They took off their shirts and vests and exposed their chests, feeling their feet sweaty and hot. They did not mention the woman. But Tom felt alone again. Last night she had asked him into her flat: it was big and had fitted white carpets and a bed with a padded white leather head-top. She wore a black filmy négligé and her kindness to Tom thickened his throat as he remembered it. He felt she had betrayed him by not being there.

And again after work they climbed up, but still there was nothing to be seen of her. Stanley kept repeating that if it was as hot as this tomorrow he wasn't going to work and that's all there was to it. But they were all there next day. By ten the temperature was in the middle seventies, and it was eighty long before noon. Harry went to the foreman to say it was impossible to work on the leads in that heat; but the foreman said there was nothing else he could put them on, and they'd have to. At midday they stood, silent, watching the skylight on her roof open, and then she slowly emerged in her white gown, holding a bundle of blankets. She looked at them, gravely, then went to the part of the roof where she was hidden from them. Tom was pleased. He felt she was more his when the other men couldn't see her. They had taken off their shirts and vests, but now they put them back again, for they felt the sun bruising their flesh. 'She must have the hide of a rhino,' said Stanley, tugging at guttering and swearing. They stopped work, and sat in the shade, moving around behind chimney stacks. A woman came to water a yellow window box just opposite them. She was middle-aged, wearing a flowered summer dress. Stanley said to her: 'We need a drink more than them.' She smiled and said: 'Better drop down to the pub quick, it'll be closing in a minute.' They exchanged pleasantries, and she left them with a smile and a wave.

'Not like Lady Godiva,' said Stanley. 'She can give us a bit of a chat and a smile.'

'You don't whistle at *her*,' said Tom, reproving.

'Listen to him,' said Stanley, 'you didn't whistle then?'

But the boy felt as if he hadn't whistled, as if only Harry and Stanley had. He was making plans, when it was time to knock off work, to get left behind and somehow make his way over to the woman. The weather report said the hot spell was due to break, so he had to move quickly. But there was no chance of being left. The other two decided to knock off work at four, because they were exhausted. As they went down, Tom quickly climbed a parapet and hoisted himself higher by pulling his weight up a chimney. He caught a glimpse of her lying on her back, her knees up, eyes closed, a brown woman lolling in the sun. He slipped and clattered down, as Stanley looked for information: 'She's gone down,' he said. He felt as if he had protected her from Stanley, and that she must be grateful to him. He could feel the bond between the woman and himself.

Next day, they stood around on the landing below the roof, reluctant to climb up into the heat. The woman who had lent Harry the blanket came out and offered them a cup of tea. They accepted gratefully, and sat around Mrs Pritchett's kitchen an hour or so, chatting. She was married to an airline pilot. A smart blonde, of about thirty, she had an eye for the handsome sharp-faced Stanley; and the two teased each other while Harry sat in a corner, watching, indulgent, though his expression reminded Stanley that he was married. And young Tom felt envious of Stanley's ease in badinage; felt, too, that Stanley's getting off with Mrs Pritchett left his romance with the woman on the roof safe and intact.

'I thought they said the heat wave'd break,' said Stanley, sullen, as the time approached when they really would have to climb up into the sunlight.

'You don't like it, then?' asked Mrs Pritchett.

'All right for some,' said Stanley. 'Nothing to do but lie about as if it was a beach up there. Do you ever go up?'

'Went up once,' said Mrs Pritchett. 'But it's a dirty place up there, and it's too hot.'

'Quite right too,' said Stanley.

Then they went up, leaving the cool neat little flat and the friendly Mrs Pritchett.

As soon as they were up they saw her. The three men looked at her, resentful at her ease in this punishing sun. Then Harry said, because of the expression on Stanley's face: 'Come on, we've got to pretend to work, at least.'

They had to wrench another length of guttering that ran beside a parapet out of its bed, so that they could replace it. Stanley took it in his two hands, tugged, swore, stood up. 'F . . . it,' he said, and sat down under a chimney. He lit a cigarette. 'F . . . them,' he said, 'what do they think we are, lizards? I've got blisters all over my hands.' Then he jumped up and climbed over the roofs and stood with his back to them. He put his fingers either side of his mouth and let out a shrill whistle. Tom and Harry squatted, not looking at each other, watching him. They could just see the woman's head, the beginnings of her brown shoulders. Stanley whistled again. Then he began stamping with his feet, and whistled and yelled and screamed at the woman, his face getting scarlet. He seemed quite mad, as he stamped and whistled, while the woman did not move, she did not move a muscle.

'Barmy,' said Tom.

'Yes,' said Harry, disapproving.

Suddenly the older man came to a decision. It was, Tom knew, to save some sort of scandal or real trouble over the woman. Harry stood up and began packing tools into a length of oily cloth. 'Stanley,' he said, commanding. At first Stanley took no notice, but Harry said: 'Stanley, we're packing it in, I'll tell Matthew.'

Stanley came back, cheeks mottled, eyes glaring.

'Can't go on like this,' said Harry. 'It'll break in a day or so. I'm going to tell Matthew we've got sunstroke, and if he doesn't like it, it's too bad.' Even Harry sounded aggrieved, Tom noted. The small, competent man, the family man with his grey hair, who was never at a loss, sounded really off balance. 'Come on,' he said, angry. He fitted himself into the open square in the roof, and went down, watching his feet on the ladder. Then Stanley went, with not a glance at the woman. Then Tom who, his throat beating with excitement, silently promised her in a backward glance: Wait for me, wait, I'm coming.

On the pavement Stanley said: 'I'm going home.' He looked white now, so perhaps he really did have sunstroke. Harry went off to find the foreman who was at work on the plumbing of some flats down the street. Tom slipped back, not into the building they had been working on, but building on whose roof the woman lay. He went straight up, no one stopping him. The skylight stood open, with an iron ladder leading up. He emerged on to the roof a couple of yards from her. She sat up, pushing back her black hair with both hands. The scarf across her breasts bound them tight, and brown flesh bulged around it. Her legs were brown and smooth. She stared at him in silence. The boy stood grinning, foolish, claiming the tenderness he expected from her.

'What do you want?' she asked.

'I . . . I came to . . . make your acquaintance,' he stammered, grinning, pleading with her.

They looked at each other, the slight, scarlet-faced excited boy, and the serious, nearly-naked woman. Then, without a word, she lay face down on her brown blanket, ignoring him.

'You like the sun, do you?' he enquired of her glistening back.

Not a word. He felt panic, thinking of how she had held him in her arms, stroked his hair, brought him where he sat, lordly, in her bed, a glass of some exhilarating liquor he had never tasted in life. He felt that if he knelt down, stroked her shoulders, her hair, she would turn and clasp him in her arms.

He said: 'The sun's all right for you, isn't it.'

She raised her head, set her chin on two small fists. 'Go away,' she said. He did not move. 'Listen,' she said, in a slow reasonable voice, where anger was kept in check, though with difficulty; looking at him, her face weary with anger: 'If you get a kick out of seeing women in bikinis, why don't you take a sixpenny bus ride to the Lido? You'd see dozens of them, without all this mountaineering.'

She hadn't understood him. He felt her unfairness pale him. He stammered: 'But I like you, I've been watching you and . . .'

'Thanks,' she said, and dropped her face again, turned away from him.

She lay there. He stood there. She said nothing. She had simply shut him out. He stood, saying nothing at all, for some minutes. He thought: She'll have to say something if I stay. But the minutes went past, with no sign of them in her, except in the tension of her back, her thighs, her arms, – the tension of waiting for him to go.

He looked up at the sky, where the sun seemed to spin in heat: and over the roofs where he and his mates had been earlier. He could see the heat quivering where they had worked. And they expect us to work in these conditions! he thought, filled with righteous indignation. The woman hadn't moved. A bit of hot wind blew her black hair softly, it shone, and was iridescent. He remembered how he had stroked it last night.

Resentment of her at last moved him off and away down the ladder, through the building, into the street. He got drunk then, in hatred of her.

Next day when he woke the sky was grey. He looked at the wet and thought, viciously: Well that's fixed you, hasn't it now? That's fixed you good and proper.

The three men were at work early on the cool leads, surrounded by damp drizzling roofs where no one came to sun themselves, black roofs, slimy with rain. Because it was cool now, they would finish the job that day, if they hurried.

Doris Lessing

Cyprian Ekwensi

Cyprian Ekwensi was born on 26th September 1921, in Minna, Nigeria, of Ibo parents. He was educated first in Nigeria at Government College, Ibadan, followed by Yaba Higher College, Achitmota College in Ghana, and the School of Forestry, Ibadan. Later he accepted a scholarship at the Chelsea School of Pharmacy, London University, where he took a professional degree.

His main career has been in journalism and broadcasting, but he has also worked as a teacher, a lecturer, a forestry officer and a chemist. He was also an active campaigner during the Biafran War, raising money for the Biafran people and the independent Biafran radio station of which he was director.

Ekwensi's interest in writing dates back to his school days in Ibadan. He has written many novels for adults and children as well as novellas, short stories and magazine articles. His work has been translated into several languages and he has travelled extensively both within and outside Nigeria.

Ekwensi's stories have popular appeal; he writes about Nigeria, the country and the people, of life in the city and in more rural areas. He believes that the writer in Africa must be committed to truth. In 1966 a volume of nine stories entitled *Loko Town and Other Stories*, including *A Stranger From Lagos*, was published and in 1968 he was awarded the *Dag Hammarskjold International Prize in Literature*.

In 1971 Cyprian Ekwensi became chairman of the East Central State Library Board, after which he became managing director of the Star Printing and Publishing Company. He wrote a weekly column for the *Daily Star* and a monthly column for a magazine called *Drum*.

In 1979 he set up a consultancy business, and was appointed managing director of *The Weekly Eagle* newspaper in 1981.

119

A Stranger From Lagos

She saw the way he looked at her when she was dancing and knew. Only a stranger would look like that at the *Umu-ogbo* dance, and only a man who had fallen would linger on her movements that way. Yet it embarrassed her when, sitting with the elderly women in the bright hot afternoon, she looked up from her sewing and saw him, asking questions. Though she knew he had seen her, he did not once look in her direction. He looked so transparently silly and pitiable.

She wondered what to do. Should she go to his help there — while her mother and her fiancé's mother were present? He seemed to be holding his own, telling fables, something about having missed his way, having recently crossed the Niger . . . . She would go to his aid. Suddenly she caught the hard look on his unsmiling face, a look full of the agony of desire.

Her legs felt too heavy to stir. Too many eyes. In Onitsha Town there were eyes on the walls. In the compound, eyes. In the streets, eyes. Such a small town, and so small-town-minded. You went down Market Street, new or old, and came back into Market Street, new or old, through a number of parallel feeder streets. Of course, Lilian had lived here since she was born and she knew her way to her lover's house without being seen even by day, and with her mother happily thinking she had gone to market. But once they saw her, once they saw a girl they knew and respected speaking with a glamorous-looking stranger like this one, or in a hotel, or standing in the streets and talking to a *man* in broad daylight, or daring to hold hands or to linger too long with a handshake, the eyes would roll and the tongues would wag and the girl's best course of action would be to leave the town or immediately be branded.

By the time Lilian looked up from her machine, he was gone. Her mother was coming back to the veranda.

'What did he say he wanted?'

'Do I know?' Her mother shrugged and made a face. 'These young men from Lagos, who understands the language they speak?'

Lilian knew he had come for her but his courage had failed him. 'Did he say his name, or where he lives?'

'He called a name. He is not of a family I know.'

Unlike her mother, Lilian cared little for 'families she knew'. She judged young men by what her instincts told her, and this time they told her she had made a conquest, full of strange enchantment. She put the scissors through the wax print and shaped it into a skirt that ended well above her knees. Her mother's eyes followed her with resentment. She called such tight clothes 'mad people's clothes'.

On her way down Market Street, Lilian wiggled in the new dress. Her hair had been newly done, and the loop earrings were large enough to play hula-hoop. Someone stopped just behind her. She looked round. Eyes. From the windows of the hotels, bookshops, sign painters, mechanics' workshops, eyes focused enquiringly on her and the stranger with such intentness that she felt like something projected on a 3-D screen for all Onitsha to view. This was sensation.

He was tall and good-looking and did not show any embarrassment at being made the spectacle of Market Street. Of course, he did not know the town. He would scandalize her, and leave her to it. That was the way of strangers. They left you to the gossips.

'I saw you in the compound — is that where you live?'

'Yes. Please, I am in a hurry. Who are you?'

'A stranger from Lagos. If you had time, I would tell you about my mission.'

'Now?' She wrinkled her nose.

'I only stopped because I saw you. It is some days now since I came to your compound. I have wanted to see you.'

'What for?' she asked unnecessarily. He did not answer.

'You're from Lagos?' Lilian said.

'Yes.'

The eyes from the hotels, bookshops, mechanical workshops, danced. A woman passer-by stopped and greeted Lilian by name. Lilian seemed to remember the face, and yet she could not place it. Her mind was focused on the stranger. 'How is your baby?' asked the passer-by. 'How is your mother ?' Lilian mumbled something . . .

'You're from Lagos,' Lilian said. 'Here in Onitsha we do not stop and talk in the streets. It is not considered respectable. It is not done by decent girls of family . . . Too many eyes . . . Wait till evening . . . .'

'Till evening, then!'

Lilian walked away. She was conscious that he was watching her. She walked down the road and beyond the roundabout into the market-stalls where they sell fish, and down the steps to the Niger. She hoped none of her mother's friends had seen her.

When she got home her mother's coldness was immediately apparent.

'Lilian, they said you were talking with a man in the street and he was holding your waist *in the street!'*

'Mama, that is impossible.'

'A strange man, they said. Wearing Western Nigeria dress — *agbada* and so on. A man who lived many years in the West.'

'Mama, he is a man of Nigeria. He only asked me the way to the post office. Mama, don't you believe the wicked gossip.'

'But you must respect yourself. You don't want to do anything that would scandalize your father's name. He is a pensioner and worked hard for his good name. You parted from your first husband. Now you have a fiancé. You are staying with me and your father. You want for nothing. Hold this your fiancé well and give him no cause to brand you.'

Lilian flashed angry eyes. 'Yes, Ma.' She bit her lips to hold back the tears.

In the evening they sat in the compound and watched the moonlight. The beams played on the banana fronds, on the pan roofs, on the mud walls. It created shadows welcomed by lovers. Whenever a car passed a fog of dust rose and obscured the street. It was a side-street and cars did not pass often.

Lilian's eyes never left the entrance to the compound. On her way back from the market she had seen her fiancé. He had been her fiancé for three years. She bore him a son, and they quarrelled and she went to live in Lagos, leaving the boy with her mother. She did not like Lagos and came back. On her return he saw how glamorous she had become and promised to make good. He bought wine and brought it to her mother saying he still wanted her. She did not much care either way. He was a trader, and his ideas about love tallied more with her mother's than her own.

All she was praying for was that the Stranger from Lagos should come quickly and leave before her fiancé arrived. Instinct warned her he might decide to come, though this was not his night. Why had she not given the Stranger a definite time? But in Onitsha love knows no definite time. Evening begins with the moonlight and ends when sleep comes.

She heard a sound outside. Her mother's voice. It was warm. She guessed it was her fiancé. He came in. She looked into his face, hard, possessive, confident. Every gesture of his showed that he owned her. Yet he had not completed the formalities. He had been at it all of three years. No one would say he was not a successful merchant.

He sat down and ordered six bottles of stout. She sat with him. She could not drink much this evening. She was sure that before the six bottles were empty something would happen. Her eyes never left the gate.

He talked. She listened. She heard a sound. It was her friend, Alice. Oh, if only they would both go out. But Alice had come, not to go out but to spend the evening, ironing clothes, plaiting her hair. She sat with them now and shared their drink. Lilian talked and laughed loudly. But it was she who heard the new sound. The Stranger was here.

To her surprise her fiancé stood up and greeted him familiarly.

'You are Mr Okonma from Lagos. I have heard of you.'

'How are you?'

'Have a drink.'

'No, thanks.'

'I don't know you as a teetotaller,' her fiancé said. He laughed, and began to explain how he met Mr Okonma once when he went to buy things in Lagos. He lived in the same street, and—

'I don't touch alcohol, Mr—

'Anya is the name.'

'I don't touch alcohol. You must be mistaken.' He sat down, gloomily, and for a moment no one said anything.

'What may be your mission in Onitsha?'

Lilian did not like the way her fiancé was pursuing the Stranger. She got up, talked to her friend. As they left, she had half her ear tuned to the conversation of the two men. To her it was conducted in an offended and offensive tone. She felt sorry and isolated though she could not be sure whether or not the two men were getting at each other.

She and Alice retired and were absorbed with their hair plaiting when the Stranger left. She went back to her fiancé's table. He was sitting alone with empty bottles before him.

'I heard about him,' he said in a high voice. 'That's why I came here this night. Isn't he one of your lovers from Lagos? When they come to Onitsha the first thing they do is to look for you.'

'I don't even know him.'

He laughed harshly but said no more. She saw his intense anger and jealousy mounting. He did not stay any longer but put on his hat and left. Lilian, puzzled, went back to Alice and resumed her plaiting.

'I have done no wrong. But I must be made to suffer all the same. Now we have quarrelled for a man I don't even know. It's like this, every day. Now he will go and mope and I will not see him for days . . .'

Alice said: 'Too many eyes in this town. They see, they don't understand and they talk . . . He should trust you more. After all, you're no kid. The other day, I was talking to a man . . .'

But Lilian was not listening. She was thinking of the Stranger from Lagos and wishing she had been braver.

Cyprian Ekwensi

Dorothy M. Johnson

Dorothy M. Johnson was born on the 19th December 1905 in McGregor, Iowa, USA. She grew up in Whitefish, Montana, and was educated at the Montana State University where she was awarded a BA degree in 1928.

Johnson began her career in publishing as a magazine editor with Gregg Publishing Co, New York (1935-1944) and then with Farrell Publishing Corporation, New York (1944-1950). She became News Editor of the *Whitefish Pilot* in 1950 where she stayed until 1953 when she was appointed Secretary/Manager of the Montana State Press Association. Following this she became Assistant Professor of Journalism at the University of Montana where she was awarded the honorary degree of Doctor of Letters in 1973. She was appointed honorary police chief of Whitefish and became an adopted member of the Blackfeet Indian Tribe in Montana with the Indian name, Kills-Both-Places.

Dorothy M. Johnson has written many novels, short stories and magazine articles, mostly about the West. Some of these, including *A Man Called Horse*, have inspired motion pictures as well as television and radio programmes. Her writing has been translated into a variety of foreign languages and has won several prestigious awards, including a *Spur Award* from the Western Writers of America in 1956, a *Levi Strauss Golden Saddleman*, and the *Western Heritage Wrangler Award*.

A Man Called Horse

He was a young man of good family, as the phrase went in the New England of a hundred-odd years ago, and the reasons for his bitter discontent were unclear, even to himself. He grew up in the gracious old Boston home under his grandmother's care, for his mother had died in giving him birth; and all his life he had known every comfort and privilege his father's wealth could provide.

But still there was the discontent, which puzzled him because he could not even define it. He wanted to live among his equals — people who were no better than he and no worse either. That was as close as he could come to describing the source of his unhappiness in Boston and his restless desire to go somewhere else.

In the year 1845 he left home and went out West, far beyond the country's creeping frontier, where he hoped to find his equals. He had the idea that in Indian country, where there was danger, all white men were kings, and he wanted to be one of them. But he found, in the West as in Boston, that the men he respected were still his superiors, even if they could not read, and those he did not respect weren't worth talking to.

He did have money, however, and he could hire the men he respected. He hired four of them, to cook and hunt and guide and be his companions, but he found them not friendly.

They were apart from him and he was still alone. He still brooded about his status in the world, longing for his equals.

On a day in June he learned what it was to have no status at all. He became a captive of a small raiding party of Crow Indians.

He heard gunfire and the brief shouts of his companions around the bend of the creek just before they died, but he never saw their bodies. He had no chance to fight because he was naked and unarmed, bathing in the creek, when a Crow warrior seized and held him.

His captor let him go at last, let him run. Then the lot of them rode him down for sport, striking him with their coup sticks. They carried the dripping scalps of his companions, and one had skinned off Baptiste's black beard as well, for a trophy.

They took him along in a matter-of-fact way, as they took the captured horses. He was unshod and naked as the horses were, and like them he had a rawhide thong round his neck. So long as he didn't fall down, the Crows ignored him.

On the second day they gave him his breeches. His feet were too swollen for his boots, but one of the Indians threw him a pair of moccasins that had belonged to the halfbreed, Henri, who was dead back at the creek. The captive wore the moccasins gratefully. The third day they let him ride one of the spare horses so the party could move faster, and on that day they came in sight of their camp.

He thought of trying to escape, hoping he might be killed in flight rather than by slow torture in the camp, but he never had a chance to try. They were more familiar with escape than he was and, knowing what to expect, they forestalled it. The only other time he had tried to escape from anyone, he had succeeded. When he had left his home in Boston, his father had raged and his grandmother had cried, but they could not talk him out of his intention.

The men of the Crow raiding party didn't bother with talk.

Before riding into camp they stopped and dressed in their regalia, and in parts of their victims' clothing; they painted their faces black. Then, leading the white man by the rawhide around his neck as though he were a horse, they rode down towards the tepee circle, shouting and singing, brandishing their weapons. He was unconscious when they got there; he fell and was dragged.

He lay dazed and battered near a tepee while the noisy, busy life of the camp swarmed around him and Indians came to stare. Thirst consumed him, and when it rained he lapped rainwater from the ground like a dog. A scrawny, shrieking, eternally busy old woman with ragged greying hair threw a chunk of meat on the grass, and he fought the dogs for it.

When his head cleared, he was angry, although anger was an emotion he knew he could not afford.

It was better when I was a horse, he thought — when they led me by the rawhide around my neck. I won't be a dog, no matter what.

The hag gave him stinking, rancid grease and let him figure out what it was for. He applied it gingerly to his bruised and sun-seared body.

Now, he thought, I smell like the rest of them.

While he was healing, he considered coldly the advantages of being a horse. A man would be humiliated, and sooner or later he would strike back and that would be the end of him. But a horse had only to be docile. Very well, he would learn to do without pride.

He understood that he was the property of the screaming old woman, a fine gift from her son, one that she liked to show off. She did more yelling at him than at anyone else, probably to impress the neighbours so they would not forget what a great and generous man her son was. She was bossy and proud, a dreadful sag of skin and bones, and she was a devilish hard worker.

The white man, who now thought of himself as a horse, forgot sometimes to worry about his danger. He kept making mental notes of things to tell his own people in Boston about this hideous adventure. He would go back a hero, and he would say, 'Grandmother, let me fetch your shawl, I've been accustomed to doing little errands for another lady about your age.'

Two girls lived in the tepee with the old hag and her warrior son. One of them, the white man concluded, was his captor's wife and the other was his little sister. The daughter-in-law was smug and spoiled. Being beloved, she did not have to be useful. The younger girl had bright, wandering eyes. Often enough they wandered to the white man who was pretending to be a horse.

The two girls worked when the old woman put them at it, but they were always running off to do something they enjoyed more. There were games and noisy contests, and there was much laughter. But not for the white man. He was finding out what loneliness could be.

That was a rich summer on the plains, with plenty of buffalo for meat and clothing and the making of tepees. The Crows were wealthy in horses, prosperous and contented. If their men had not been so avid for glory, the white man thought, there would have been a lot more of them. But they went out of their way to court death, and when one of them met it, the whole camp mourned extravagantly and cried to their God for vengeance.

The captive was a horse all summer, a docile bearer of burdens, careful and patient. He kept reminding himself that he had to be better-natured than other horses, because he could not lash out with hoofs or teeth. Helping the old woman load up the horses for travel, he yanked at a pack and said, 'Whoa, brother. It goes easier when you don't fight.'

The horse gave him a big-eyed stare as if it understood his language — a comforting thought, because nobody else did. But even among the horses he felt unequal. They were able to look out for themselves if they escaped. He would simply starve. He was envious still, even among the horses.

Humbly he fetched and carried. Sometimes he even offered to help, but he had not the skill for the endless work of the women, and he was not trusted to hunt with the men, the providers.

When the camp moved he carried a pack, trudging with the women. Even the dogs worked then, pulling small burdens on travois of sticks.

The Indian who had captured him lived like a lord, as he had a right to do. He hunted with his peers, attended long ceremonial meetings with much chanting and dancing, and lounged in the shade with his smug bride. He had only two responsibilities: to kill buffalo and to gain glory. The white man was so far beneath him in status that the Indian did not even think of envy.

One day several things happened that made the captive think he might sometime become a man again. That was the day when he began to understand their language. For four months he had heard it, day and night, the joy and the mourning, the ritual chanting and sung prayers, the squabbles and the deliberations. None of it meant anything to him at all.

But on that important day in early fall the two young women set out for the river, and one of them called over her shoulder to the old woman. The white man was startled. She had said she was going to bathe. His understanding was so sudden that he felt as if his ears had come unstopped. Listening to the racket of the camp, he heard fragments of meaning instead of gabble.

On that same important day the old woman brought a pair of new moccasins out of the tepee and tossed them on the ground before him. He could not believe she would do anything for him because of kindness, but giving him moccasins was one way of looking after her property.

In thanking her, he dared greatly. He picked a little handful of fading fall flowers and took them to her as she squatted in front of her tepee, scraping a buffalo hide with a tool made from a piece of iron tied to a bone. Her hands were hideous — most of the fingers had the first joint missing. He bowed solemnly and offered the flowers.

She glared at him from beneath the short, ragged tangle of her hair. She stared at the flowers, knocked them out of his hand and went running to the next tepee, squalling the story. He heard her and the other women screaming with laughter.

The white man squared his shoulders and walked boldy over to watch three small boys shooting arrows at a target. He said in English, 'Show me how to do that, will you?'

They frowned, but he held out his hand as if there could be no doubt. One of them gave him a bow and one arrow, and they snickered when he missed.

The people were easily amused, except when they were angry. They were amused at him, playing with the little boys. A few days later he asked the hag, with gestures, for a bow that her son had just discarded, a man-sized bow of horn. He scavenged for old arrows. The old woman cackled at his marksmanship and called her neighbours to enjoy the fun.

When he could understand words, he could identify his people by their names. The old woman was Greasy Hand, and her daughter was Pretty Calf. The other young woman's name was not clear to him, for the words were not in his vocabulary. The man who had captured him was Yellow Robe.

Once he could understand, he could begin to talk a little, and then he was less lonely. Nobody had been able to see any reason for talking to him, since he would not understand anyway. He asked the old woman, 'What is my name?' Until he knew it, he was incomplete. She shrugged to let him know he had none.

He told her in the Crow language, 'My name is Horse.' He repeated it, and she nodded. After that they called him Horse when they called him anything. Nobody cared except the white man himself.

They trusted him enough to let him stray out of camp, so that he might have got away and, by unimaginable good luck, reached a trading post or a fort, but winter was too close. He did not dare leave without a horse; he needed clothing and a better hunting weapon than he had, and more certain skill in using it. He did not dare steal, for then they would surely have pursued him, and just as certainly they would have caught him. Remembering the warmth of the home that was waiting in Boston, he settled down for the winter.

On a cold night he crept into the tepee after the others had gone to bed. Even a horse might try to find shelter from the wind. The old woman grumbled, but without conviction. She did not put him out.

They tolerated him, back in the shadows, so long as he did not get in the way.

He began to understand how the family that owned him differed from the others. Fate had been cruel to them. In a short, sharp argument among the old women, one of them derided Greasy Hand by sneering, 'You have no relatives!' and Greasy Hand raved for minutes of the deeds of her father and uncles and brothers. And she had had four sons, she reminded her detractor — who answered with scorn, 'Where are they?'

Later the white man found her moaning and whimpering to herself, rocking back and forth on her haunches, staring at her mutilated hands. By that time he understood. A mourner often chopped off a finger joint. Old Greasy Hand had mourned often. For the first time he felt a twinge of pity, but he put it aside as another emotion, like anger, that he could not afford. He thought: what tales I will tell when I get home.

He wrinkled his nose in disdain. The camp stank of animals and meat and rancid grease. He looked down at his naked, shivering legs and was startled, remembering that he was still only a horse.

He could not trust the old woman. She fed him only because a starved slave would die and not be worth boasting about. Just how fitful her temper was he saw on the day when she got tired of stumbling over one of the hundred dogs that infested the camp. This was one of her own dogs, a large, strong one that pulled a baggage travois when the tribe moved camp.

Countless times he had seen her kick at the beast as it lay sleeping in front of the tepee, in her way. The dog always moved, with a yelp, but it always got in the way again. One day she gave the dog its usual kick and then stood scolding at it while the animal rolled its eyes sleepily. The old woman suddenly picked up her axe and cut the dog's head off with one blow. Looking well satisfied with herself, she beckoned her slave to remove the body.

It could have been me, he thought, if I were a dog. But I'm a horse.

His hope of life lay with the girl, Pretty Calf. He set about courting her, realizing how desperately poor he was both in property and honour. He owned no horse, no weapon but the old bow and the battered arrows. He had nothing to give away, and he needed gifts, because he did not dare seduce the girl.

One of the customs of courtship involved sending a gift of horses to a girl's older brother and bestowing much buffalo meat upon her mother. The white man could not wait for some far-off time when he might have either horses or meat to give away. And his courtship had to be secret. It was not for him to stroll past the groups of watchful girls, blowing a flute made of an eagle's wing bone, as the flirtatious young bucks did.

He could not ride past Pretty Calf's tepee, painted and bedizened: he had no horse, no finery.

Back home, he remembered, I could marry just about any girl I'd wanted to. But he wasted little time thinking about that. A future was something to be earned.

The most he dared do was wink at Pretty Calf now and then, or state his admiration while she giggled and hid her face. The least he dared do to win his bride was to elope with her, but he had to give her a horse to put the seal of tribal approval on that. And he had no horse until he killed a man to get one . . .

His opportunity came in early spring. He was casually accepted by that time. He did not belong, but he was amusing to the Crows, like a strange pet, or they would not have fed him through the winter.

His chance came when he was hunting small game with three young boys who were his guards as well as his scornful companions. Rabbits and birds were of no account in a camp well fed on buffalo meat, but they made good targets.

His party walked far that day. All of them at once saw the two horses in a sheltered coulee. The boys and the man crawled forward on their bellies, and then they saw an Indian who lay on the ground, moaning, a lone traveller. From the way the boys inched eagerly forward, Horse knew the man was fair prey — a member of some enemy tribe.

This is the way the captive white man acquired wealth and honour to win a bride and save his life: he shot an arrow into the sick man, a split second ahead of one of his small companions, and dashed forward to strike the still-groaning man with his bow, to count first coup. Then he seized the hobbled horses.

By the time he had the horses secure and with them his hope for freedom, the boys had followed, counting coup with gestures and shrieks they had practised since boyhood, and one of them had the scalp. The white man was grimly amused to see the boy double up with sudden nausea when he had the thing in his hand . . .

There was a hubbub in the camp when they rode in that evening, two of them on each horse. The captive was noticed. Indians who had ignored him as a slave stared at the brave man who had struck first coup and had stolen horses.

The hubbub lasted all night, as fathers boasted loudly of their young sons' exploits. The white man was called upon to settle an argument between two fierce boys as to which of them had struck second coup and which must be satisfied with third. After much talk that went over his head, he solemnly pointed at the nearest boy. He didn't know which boy it was and didn't care, but the boy did.

The white man had watched warriors in their triumph. He knew what to do. Modesty about achievements had no place among the Crow people. When a man did something big, he told about it.

The white man smeared his face with grease and charcoal. He walked inside the tepee circle, chanting and singing. He used his own language.

'You heathens, you savages,' he shouted. 'I'm going to get out of here someday! I am going to get away!' The Crow people listened respectfully. In the Crow tongue he shouted, 'Horse! I am Horse!' and they nodded.

He had a right to boast and he had two horses. Before dawn the white man and his bride were sheltered beyond a far hill, and he was telling her, 'I love you, little lady. I love you.'

She looked at him with her great dark eyes, and he thought she understood his English words — or as much as she needed to understand.

'You are my treasure,' he said, 'more precious than jewels, better than fine gold. I am going to call you Freedom.'

When they returned to camp two days later, he was bold but worried. His ace, he suspected, might not be high enough in the game he was playing without being sure of the rules. But it served.

Old Greasy Hand raged — but not at him. She complained loudly that her daughter had let herself go too cheap. But the marriage was as good as any Crow marriage. He had paid a horse.

He learned the language faster after that, from Pretty Calf, whom he sometimes called Freedom. He learned that his attentive, adoring bride was fourteen years old.

One thing he had not guessed was the difference that being Pretty Calf's husband would make in his relationship to her mother and brother. He had hoped only to make his position a little safer, but he had not expected to be treated with dignity. Greasy Hand no longer spoke to him at all. When the white man spoke to her, his bride murmured in dismay, explaining at great length that he must never do that. There could be no conversation between a man and his mother-in-law. He could not even mention a word that was part of her name.

Having improved his status so magnificently, he felt no need for hurry in getting away. Now that he had a woman he had as good a chance to be rich as any man. Pretty Calf waited on him; she seldom ran off to play games with other young girls, but took pride in learning from her mother the many women's skills of tanning hides and making clothing and preparing food.

He was no more a horse but a kind of man, a half-Indian, still poor and unskilled but laden with honours, clinging to the buckskin fringes of Crow society.

Escape could wait until he could manage it in comfort, with fit clothing and a good horse, with hunting weapons. Escape could wait until the camp moved near some trading post. He did not plan how he would get home. He dreamed of being there all at once and of telling stories nobody would believe. There was no hurry.

Pretty Calf delighted in educating him. He began to understand tribal arrangements, customs and why things were as they were. They were that way because they had always been so. His young wife giggled when she told him, in his ignorance, things she had always known. But she did not laugh when her brother's wife was taken by another warrior. She explained that solemnly with words and signs.

Yellow Robe belonged to a society called the Big Dogs. The wife-stealer, Cut Neck, belonged to the Foxes. They were fellow tribesmen: they hunted together and fought side by side, but men of one society could take away wives from the other society if they wished, subject to certain limitations.

When Cut Neck rode up to the tepee, laughing and singing, and called to Yellow Robe's wife, 'Come out! Come out!' she did as ordered, looking smug as usual, meek and entirely willing. Thereafter she rode beside him in ceremonial processions and carried his coup stick, while his other wife pretended not to care.

'But why?' the white man demanded of his wife, his Freedom. 'Why did our brother let his woman go? He sits and smokes and does not speak.'

Pretty Calf was shocked at the suggestion. Her brother could not possibly reclaim his woman, she explained. He could not even let her come back if she wanted to — and she probably would want to when Cut Neck tired of her. Yellow Robe could not even admit that his heart was sick. That was the way things were. Deviation meant dishonour.

The woman could have hidden from Cut Neck, she said. She could even have refused to go with him if she had been *ba-wurokee* — a really virtuous woman. But she had been his woman before, for a little while on a berrying expedition, and he had a right to claim her.

There was no sense in it the white man insisted. He glared at his young wife. 'If you go, I will bring you back,' he promised.

She laughed and buried her head against his shoulder. 'I will not have to go,' she said. 'Horse is my first man. There is no hole in my moccasin.'

He stroked her hair and said, '*Ba-wurokee.*'

With great daring, she murmured, '*Hayha,*' and when he did not answer, because he did not know what she meant, she drew away, hurt.

'A woman calls her man that if she thinks he will not leave her. Am I wrong?'

The white man held her closer and lied. 'Pretty Calf is not wrong. Horse will not leave her. Horse will not take another woman, either.' No, he certainly would not. Parting from this one was going to be harder than getting her had been. '*Hayha,*' he murmured. 'Freedom'.

His conscience irked him, but not very much. Pretty Calf could get another man easily enough when he was gone, and a better provider. His hunting skill was improving, but he was still awkward.

There was no hurry about leaving. He was used to most of the Crow ways and could stand the rest. He was becoming prosperous. He owned five horses. His place in the life of the tribe was secure, such as it was. Three or four young women, including the one who had belonged to Yellow Robe, made advances to him. Pretty Calf took pride in the fact that her man was so attractive.

By the time he had what he needed for a secret journey, the grass grew yellow on the plains and the long cold was close. He was enslaved by the girl he called Freedom and, before the winter ended, by the knowledge that she was carrying his child . . .

The Big Dog society held a long ceremony in the spring. The white man strolled with his woman along the creek bank thinking: when I get home I will tell them about the chants and the drumming. Sometime. Sometime.

Pretty Calf would not go to bed when they went back to the tepee.

'Wait and find out about my brother,' she urged. 'Something may happen.'

So far as Horse could figure out, the Big Dogs were having some kind of election. He pampered his wife by staying up with her by the fire. Even the old woman, who was a great one for getting sleep when she was not working, prowled around restlessly.

The white man was yawning by the time the noise of the ceremony died down. When Yellow Robe strode in, garish and heathen in his paint and feathers and furs, the women cried out. There was conversation, too fast for Horse to follow, and the old woman wailed once, but her son silenced her with a gruff command.

When the white man went to sleep he thought his wife was weeping beside him.

The next morning she explained.

'He wears the bearskin belt. Now he can never retreat in battle. He will always be in danger. He will die.'

Maybe he wouldn't, the white man tried to convince her. Pretty Calf recalled that some few men had been honoured by the bearskin belt, vowed to the highest daring, and had not died. If they lived through the summer, then they were free of it.

'My brother wants to die,' she mourned. 'His heart is bitter.'

Yellow Robe lived through half a dozen clashes with small parties of raiders from hostile tribes. His honours were many. He captured horses in any enemy camp, led two successful raids, counted first coup and snatched a gun from the hand of an enemy tribesman. He wore wolf tails on his moccasins and ermine skins on his shirt, and he fringed his leggings with scalps in token of his glory.

When his mother ventured to suggest, as she did many times, 'My son should take a new wife, I need another woman to help me,' he ignored her. He spent much time in prayer, alone in the hills or in conference with a medicine man. He fasted and made vows and kept them. And before he could be free of the heavy honour of the bearskin belt, he went on his last raid.

The warriors were returning from the north just as the white man and two other hunters approached from the south, with buffalo and elk meat dripping from the bloody hides tied on their restive ponies. One of the hunters grunted, and they stopped to watch a rider on the hill north of the tepee circle.

The rider dismounted, held up a blanket and dropped it. He

repeated the gesture.

The hunters murmured dismay. 'Two! Two men dead!' They rode fast into the camp, where there was already wailing.

A messenger came down from the war party on the hill. The rest of the party delayed to paint their faces for mourning and for victory. One of the two dead men was Yellow Robe. They had put his body in a cave and walled it in with rocks. The other man died later, and his body was in a tree.

There was blood on the ground before the tepee to which Yellow Robe would return no more. His mother, with her hair chopped short, sat in the doorway, rocking back and forth on her haunches, wailing her heartbreak. She cradled one mutilated hand in the other. She had cut off another finger joint.

Pretty Calf had cut off chunks of her long hair and was crying as she gashed her arms with a knife. The white man tried to take the knife away, but she protested so piteously that he let her do as she wished. He was sickened with the lot of them.

Savages! he thought. Now I will go back! I'll go hunting alone, and I'll keep on going.

But he did not go just yet, because he was the only hunter in the lodge of the two grieving women, one of them old and the other pregnant with his child.

In their mourning they made him a pauper again. Everything that meant comfort, wealth and safety they sacrificed to the spirits because of the death of Yellow Robe. The tepee, made of seventeen fine buffalo hides, the furs that should have kept them warm, the white deerskin dress trimmed with elk teeth that Pretty Calf loved so well, even their tools and Yellow Robe's weapons — everything but his sacred medicine objects — they left there on the prairie, and the whole camp moved away. Two of his best horses were killed as a sacrifice, and the women gave away the rest.

They had no shelter. They would have no tepee of their own for two months at least of mourning, and then the women would have to tan hides to make it. Meanwhile they could live in temporary huts made of willows, covered with skins given them in pity by their friends. They could have lived with relatives, but Yellow Robe's women had no relatives.

The white man had not realized until then how terrible a thing it was for Crow to have no kinfolk. No wonder old Greasy Hand had only stumps for fingers. She had mourned from one year to the next for everyone she had ever loved. She had no one left but her daughter, Pretty Calf.

Horse was furious at their foolishness. It had been bad enough for him, a captive, to be naked as a horse and poor as a slave, but that was because his captors had stripped him. These women had voluntarily given up everything they needed.

He was too angry at them to sleep in the willow hut. He lay under a sheltering tree. And on the third night of the mourning he made his plans. He had a knife and a bow. He would go after meat, taking two horses. And he would not come back. There were, he realized, many things he was not going to tell when he got back home.

In the willow hut, Pretty Calf cried out. He heard rustling there, and the old woman's querulous voice.

Some twenty hours later his son was born, two months early, in the tepee of a skilled medicine woman. The child was born without breath, and the mother died before the sun went down.

The white man was too shocked to think whether he should mourn, or how he should mourn. The old woman screamed until she was voiceless. Piteously she approached him, bent and trembling, blind with grief. She held out her knife and he took it.

She spread out her hands and shook her head. If she cut off any more finger joints, she could do no more work. She could not afford any more lasting signs of grief.

The white man said, 'All right! All right!' between his teeth.

He hacked his arms with the knife and stood watching the blood run down. It was little enough to do for Pretty Calf, for little Freedom.

Now there is nothing to keep me, he realized. When I get home, I must not let them see the scars.

He looked at Greasy Hand, hideous in her grief-burdened age, and thought: I really am free now! When a wife dies, her husband has no more duty towards her family. Pretty Calf had told him so, long ago, when he wondered why a certain man moved out of one tepee and into another.

The old woman, of course, would be a scavenger. There was one other with the tribe, an ancient crone who had no relatives, toward whom no one felt any responsibility. She lived on food thrown away by the more fortunate. She slept in shelters that she built with her own knotted hands. She plodded wearily at the end of the procession when the camp moved. When she stumbled, nobody cared. When she died, nobody would miss her.

Tomorrow morning, the white man decided, I will go.

His mother-in-law's sunken mouth quivered. She said one word, questioningly. She said, *'Eero-oshay?'* She said, 'Son?'

Blinking, he remembered. When a wife died, her husband was free. But her mother, who had ignored him with dignity, might if she wished ask him to stay. She invited him by calling him Son, and he accepted by answering Mother.

Greasy Hand stood before him, bowed with years, withered with unceasing labour, loveless and childless, scarred with grief. But with all her burdens she still loved life enough to beg it from him, the only person she had any right to ask. She was stripping herself of all she had left, her pride.

He looked eastward across the prairie. Two thousand miles away was home. The old woman would not live forever. He could afford to wait, for he was young. He could afford to be magnanimous, for he knew he was a man. He gave her the answer. *'Eegya,'* he said. 'Mother.'

He went home three years later. He explained no more than to say, 'I lived with Crows for a while. It was some time before I could leave. They called me Horse.'

He did not find it necessary either to apologize or to boast, because he was the equal of any man on earth.

Dorothy M. Johnson

Roald Dahl

Roald Dahl was born in 1916 at Llandaff, Glamorgan, the son of Norwegian parents, and was educated at Repton school in Derbyshire. As a young man he joined an expedition to explore the interior of Newfoundland, and on his return he started work at the Shell Oil Company in London. In 1938 he was sent to Dar es Salaam, but at the outbreak of the Second World War in 1939 he enlisted in the RAF in Nairobi. He was seriously injured after joining a fighter squadron in Libya, but later saw further active service as a fighter pilot in Syria and Greece.

In 1942 Dahl went to Washington as Assistant Air Attaché and soon after this he began to write stories. Later in the war he worked for Intelligence and by 1945 he had been promoted to Wing Commander.

Roald Dahl's first twelve stories are based on his war time experiences, and are collected in one volume entitled *Over To You*. Since then he has written a huge number of short stories and novels for adults and children alike. Perhaps his most famous children's book, *Charlie and the Chocolate Factory*, was published in 1964. Since then it has sold millions of copies and has been translated into fifteen different languages. His other books for children have won many awards and have become international best sellers.

Roald Dahl died in 1998.

The Hitch-hiker

I had a new car. It was an exciting toy, a big B.M.W. 3.3 Li, which means 3.3 litre, long wheelbase, fuel injection. It had a top speed of 129 m.p.h and terrific acceleration. The body was pale blue. The seats inside were darker blue and they were made of leather, genuine soft leather of the finest quality. The windows were electrically operated and so was the sunroof. The radio aerial popped up when I switched on the radio, and disappeared when I switched it off. The powerful engine growled and grunted impatiently at slow speeds, but at sixty miles an hour the growling stopped and the motor began to purr with pleasure.

I was driving up to London by myself. It was a lovely June day. They were haymaking in the fields and there were buttercups along both sides of the road. I was whispering along at seventy miles an hour, leaning back comfortably in my seat, with no more than a couple of fingers resting lightly on the wheel to keep her steady. Ahead of me I saw a man thumbing a lift. I touched the footbrake and brought the car to a stop beside him. I always stopped for hitch-hikers. I knew just how it used to feel to be standing on the side of a country road watching the cars go by. I hated the drivers for pretending they didn't see me, especially the ones in big cars with three empty seats. The large expensive cars seldom stopped. It was always the smaller ones that offered you a lift, or the old rusty ones, or the ones that were already crammed full of children and the driver would say, 'I think we can squeeze in one more.'

The hitch-hiker poked his head through the open window and said, 'Going to London, guv'nor?'

'Yes,' I said. 'Jump in.'

He got in and I drove on.

He was a small ratty-faced man with grey teeth. His eyes were dark and quick and clever, like a rat's eyes, and his ears were slightly pointed at the top. He had a cloth cap on his head and he was wearing a greyish-coloured jacket with enormous pockets. The grey jacket, together with the quick eyes and the pointed ears, made him look more than anything like some sort of a huge human rat

'What part of London are you headed for?' I asked him.

'I'm goin' right through London and out the other side,' he said. 'I'm goin' to Epsom, for the races. It's Derby Day today.'

'So it is,' I said. 'I wish I were going with you. I love betting on horses.'

'I never bet on horses,' he said. 'I don't even watch 'em run. That's a stupid silly business.'

'Then why do you go?' I asked.

He didn't seem to like that question. His little ratty face went absolutely blank and he sat there staring straight ahead at the road, saying nothing.

'I expect you help to work the betting machines or something like that,' I said.

'That's even sillier,' he answered. 'There's no fun working them lousy machines and selling tickets to mugs. Any fool could do that.'

There was a long silence. I decided not to question him any more. I remembered how irritated I used to get in my hitch-hiking days when drivers kept asking *me* questions. Where are you going? Why are you going there? What's your job? Are you married? Do you have a girlfriend? What's her name? How old are you? And so on and so forth. I used to hate it.

'I'm sorry,' I said. 'It's none of my business what you do. The trouble is, I'm a writer, and most writers are terribly nosy parkers.'

'You write books?' he asked.

'Yes.'

'Writin' books is OK,' he said. 'It's what I call a skilled trade. I'm in a skilled trade too. The folks I despise is them that spend all their lives doin' crummy old routine jobs with no skill in 'em at all. You see what I mean?'

'Yes.'

'The secret of life,' he said, 'is to become very very good at somethin' that's very very 'ard to do.'

'Like you,' I said.

'Exactly. You and me both.'

'What makes you think that *I'm* any good at my job?' I asked. 'There's an awful lot of bad writers around.'

143

'You wouldn't be drivin' about in a car like this if you weren't no good at it,' he answered. 'It must've cost a tidy packet, this little job.'

'It wasn't cheap.'

'What can she do flat out?' he asked.

'One hundred and twenty-nine miles an hour,' I told him.

'I'll bet she won't do it.'

'I'll bet she will.'

'All car makers is liars,' he said. 'You can buy any car you like and it'll never do what the makers say it will in the ads.'

'This one will.'

'Open 'er up then and prove it,' he said. 'Go on, guv'nor, open 'er right up and let's see what she'll do.'

There is a roundabout at Chalfont St Peter and immediately beyond it there's a long straight section of dual carriageway. We came out of the roundabout on to the carriageway and I pressed my foot down on the accelerator. The big car leaped forward as though she'd been stung. In ten seconds or so, we were doing ninety.

'Lovely!' he cried. 'Beautiful! Keep goin'!'

I had the accelerator jammed right down against the floor and I held it there.

'One hundred!' he shouted . . . 'A hundred and five! . . . A hundred and ten! . . . A hundred and fifteen! Go on! Don't slack off!'

I was in the outside lane and we flashed past several cars as though they were standing still — a green Mini, a big cream-coloured Citroën, a white Land-Rover, a huge truck with a container on the back, an orange-coloured Volkswagen Minibus . . .

'A hundred and twenty!' my passenger shouted, jumping up and down. 'Go on! Go on! Get 'er up to one-two-nine!'

At that moment, I heard the scream of a police siren. It was so loud it seemed to be right inside the car, and then a policeman on a motorcycle loomed up alongside us on the inside lane and went past us and raised a hand for us to stop.

'Oh, my sainted aunt!' I said. 'That's torn it!'

The policeman must have been doing about a hundred and thirty when he passed us, and he took plenty of time slowing down. Finally, he pulled into the side of the road and I pulled in behind him. 'I didn't know police motorcycles could go as fast as that,' I said rather lamely.

'That one can,' my passenger said. 'It's the same make as yours. It's a B.M.W. R90S. Fastest bike on the road. That's what they're usin' nowadays.'

The policeman got off his motorcycle and leaned the machine sideways on to its prop stand. Then he took off his gloves and placed them carefully on the seat. He was in no hurry now. He had us where he wanted us and he knew it.

'This is real trouble,' I said. 'I don't like it one bit.'

'Don't talk to 'im any more than is necessary, you understand,' my companion said. 'Just sit tight and keep mum.'

Like an executioner approaching his victim, the policeman came strolling slowly towards us. He was a big meaty man with a belly, and his blue breeches were skintight around his enormous thighs. His goggles were pulled up on to the helmet, showing a smouldering red face with wide cheeks.

We sat there like guilty schoolboys, waiting for him to arrive.

'Watch out for this man,' my passenger whispered. ' 'Ee looks mean as the devil.'

The policeman came round to my open window and placed one meaty hand on the sill. 'What's the hurry?' he said.

'No hurry, officer,' I answered.

'Perhaps there's a woman in the back having a baby and you're rushing her to hospital? Is that it?'

'No, officer.'

'Or perhaps your house is on fire and you're dashing home to rescue the family from upstairs?' His voice was dangerously soft and mocking.

'My house isn't on fire, officer.'

'In that case,' he said, 'you've got yourself into a nasty mess, haven't you? Do you know what the speed limit is in this country?'

'Seventy,' I said.

'And do you mind telling me exactly what speed you were doing just now?'

I shrugged and didn't say anything.

When he spoke next, he raised his voice so loud that I jumped. '*One hundred and twenty miles per hour!*' he barked. 'That's *fifty* miles an hour over the limit!'

He turned his head and spat out a big gob of spit. It landed on the wing of my car and started sliding down over my beautiful blue paint. Then he turned back again and stared hard at my passenger. 'And who are you?' he asked sharply.

'He's a hitch-hiker,' I said. 'I'm giving him a lift.'

'I didn't ask you,' he said. 'I asked him.'

' 'Ave I done somethin' wrong?' my passenger asked. His voice was as soft and oily as haircream.

'That's more than likely,' the policeman answered. 'Anyway, you're a witness. I'll deal with you in a minute. Driving licence,' he snapped, holding out his hand.

I gave him my driving licence.

He unbuttoned the left-hand breast-pocket of his tunic and brought out the dreaded book of tickets. Carefully, he copied the name and address from my licence. Then he gave it back to me. He strolled round to the front of the car and read the number from the numberplate and wrote that down as well. He filled in the date, the time and the details of my offence. Then he tore out the top copy of the ticket. But before handing it to me, he checked that all the information had come through clearly on his own carbon copy. Finally, he replaced the book in his tunic pocket and fastened the button.

'Now you,' he said to my passenger, and he walked around to the other side of the car. From the other breast-pocket he produced a small black notebook. 'Name?' he snapped.

'Michael Fish,' my passenger said.

'Address?'

'Fourteen, Windsor Lane, Luton.'

'Show me something to prove this is your real name and address,' the policeman said.

My passenger fished in his pockets and came out with a driving licence of his own. The policeman checked the name and address and handed it back to him. 'What's your job?' he asked sharply.

'I'm an 'od carrier.'

'A *what*?'

'An 'od carrier.'

'Spell it.'

'H-O-D C-A- . . .'

'That'll do. And what's a hod carrier, may I ask?'

'An 'od carrier, officer, is a person 'oo carries the cement up the ladder to the bricklayer. And the 'od is what 'ee carries it in. It's got a long 'andle, and on the top you've got two bits of wood set at an angle . . .'

'All right, all right. Who's your employer?'

'Don't 'ave one. I'm unemployed.'

The policeman wrote all this down in the black notebook. Then he returned the book to its pocket and did up the button.

'When I get back to the station I'm going to do a little checking up on you,' he said to my passenger.

'Me? What've I done wrong?' the rat-faced man asked.

'I don't like your face, that's all,' the policeman said. 'And we just might have a picture of it somewhere in our files.' He strolled round the car and returned to my window.

'I suppose you know you're in serious trouble,' he said to me.

'Yes, officer.'

'You won't be driving this fancy car of yours again for a very long time, not after *we've* finished with you. You won't be driving *any* car again come to that for several years. And a good thing, too. I hope they lock you up for a spell into the bargain.'

'You mean prison?' I asked, alarmed.

'Absolutely,' he said, smacking his lips. 'In the clink. Behind the bars. Along with all the other criminals who break the law. *And* a hefty fine into the bargain. Nobody will be more pleased about that than me. I'll see you in court, both of you. You'll be getting a summons to appear.'

He turned away and walked over to his motorcycle. He flipped the prop stand back into position with his foot and swung his leg over the saddle. Then he kicked the starter and roared off up the road out of sight.

'Phew!' I gasped. 'That's done it.'

'We was caught,' my passenger said. 'We was caught good and proper.'

'I was caught, you mean.'

'That's right,' he said. 'What you goin' to do now, guv'nor?'

'I'm going straight up to London to talk to my solicitor,' I said. I started the car and drove on.

'You mustn't believe what 'ee said to you about goin' to prison,' my passenger said. 'They don't put nobody in the clink just for speedin'.'

'Are you sure of that?' I asked.

'I'm positive,' he answered. 'They can take your licence away and they can give you a whoppin' big fine, but that'll be the end of it.'

I felt tremendously relieved.

'By the way,' I said, 'why did you lie to him?'

'Who, me?' he said. 'What makes you think I lied?'

'You told him you were an unemployed hod carrier. But you told *me* you were in a highly skilled trade.'

'So I am,' he said. 'But it don't pay to tell everythin' to a copper.'

'So what *do* you do?' I asked him.

'Ah,' he said slyly. 'That'd be tellin', wouldn't it?'

'Is it something you're ashamed of?'

'Ashamed?' he cried. 'Me, ashamed of my job? I'm about as proud of it as anybody could be in the entire world!'

'Then why won't you tell me?'

'You writers really is nosy parkers, aren't you?' he said. 'And you ain't goin' to be 'appy, I don't think, until you've found out exactly what the answer is?'

'I don't really care one way or the other,' I told him, lying.

He gave me a crafty little ratty look out of the sides of his eyes. 'I think you do care,' he said. 'I can see it on your face that you think I'm in some kind of a very peculiar trade and you're just achin' to know what it is.'

I didn't like the way he read my thoughts. I kept quiet and stared at the road ahead.

'You'd be right, too,' he went on. 'I *am* in a very peculiar trade. I'm in the queerest peculiar trade of 'em all.'

I waited for him to go on.

'That's why I 'as to be extra careful 'oo I'm talkin' to, you see. 'Ow am I to know, for instance, you're not another copper in plain clothes?'

'Do I look like a copper?'

'No,' he said. 'You don't. And you ain't. Any fool could tell that.'

He took from his pocket a tin of tobacco and a packet of cigarette papers and started to roll a cigarette. I was watching him out of the corner of one eye, and the speed with which he performed this rather difficult operation was incredible. The cigarette was rolled and ready in about five seconds. He ran his tongue along the edge of the paper, stuck it down and popped the cigarette between his lips. Then, as if from nowhere, a lighter appeared in his hand. The lighter flamed. The cigarette was lit. The lighter disappeared. It was altogether a remarkable performance.

'I've never seen anyone roll a cigarette as fast as that,' I said.

'Ah,' he said, taking a deep suck of smoke. 'So you noticed.'

'Of course I noticed. It was quite fantastic.'

He sat back and smiled. It pleased him very much that I had noticed how quickly he could roll a cigarette. 'You want to know what

148

makes me able to do it?' he asked.

'Go on then.'

'It's because I've got fantastic fingers. These fingers of mine,' he said, holding up both hands high in front of him, 'are quicker and cleverer than the fingers of the best piano player in the world!'

'Are you a piano player?'

'Don't be daft,' he said. 'Do I look like a piano player?'

I glanced at his fingers. They were so beautifully shaped, so slim and long and elegant, they didn't seem to belong to the rest of him at all. They looked more like the fingers of a brain surgeon or a watchmaker.

'My job,' he went on, 'is a hundred times more difficult than playin' the piano. Any twerp can learn to do that. There's titchy little kids learnin' to play the piano in almost any 'ouse you go into these days. That's right, ain't it?'

'More or less,' I said.

'Of course it's right. But there's not one person in ten million can learn to do what I do. Not one in ten million! 'Ow about that?'

'Amazing,' I said.

'You're darn right it's amazin', ' he said.

'I think I know what you do,' I said. 'You do conjuring tricks. You're a conjurer.'

'Me?' he snorted. 'A conjurer? Can you picture me goin' round crummy kids' parties makin' rabbits come out of top 'ats?'

'Then you're a card player. You get people into card games and deal yourself marvellous hands.'

'Me! A rotten cardsharper!' he cried. 'That's a miserable racket if ever there was one.'

'All right. I give up.'

I was taking the car along slowly now, at no more than forty miles an hour, to make quite sure I wasn't stopped again. We had come on to the main London-Oxford road and were running down the hill towards Denham.

Suddenly, my passenger was holding up a black leather belt in his hand. 'Ever seen this before?' he asked. The belt had a brass buckle of unusual design.

'Hey!' I said. 'That's mine, isn't it? It *is* mine! Where did you get it?'

He grinned and waved the belt gently from side to side. 'Where d'you think I got it?' he said. 'Off the top of your trousers, of course.'

I reached down and felt for my belt. It was gone.

'You mean you took it off me while we've been driving along?' I asked, flabbergasted.

He nodded, watching me all the time with those little black ratty eyes.

'That's impossible,' I said. 'You'd have had to undo the buckle and slide the whole thing out through the loops all the way round. I'd have seen you doing it. And even if I hadn't seen you, I'd have felt it.'

'Ah, but you didn't, did you?' he said, triumphant. He dropped the belt on his lap, and now all at once there was a brown shoelace dangling from his fingers. 'And what about this, then?' he exclaimed, waving the shoelace.

'What about it?' I said.

'Anyone around 'ere missin' a shoelace?' he asked, grinning.

I glanced down at my shoes. The lace of one of them was missing. 'Good grief!' I said. 'How did you do that? I never saw you bending down.'

'You never saw nothin', ' he said proudly. 'You never even saw me move an inch. And you know why?'

'Yes,' I said. 'Because you've got fantastic fingers.'

'Exactly right!' he cried. 'You catch on pretty quick, don't you?' He sat back and sucked away at his home-made cigarette, blowing the smoke out in a thin stream against the windshield. He knew he had impressed me greatly with those two tricks, and this made him very happy. 'I don't want to be late,' he said. 'What time is it?'

'There's a clock in front of you,' I told him.

'I don't trust car clocks,' he said. 'What does your watch say?'

I hitched up my sleeve to look at the watch on my wrist. It wasn't there. I looked at the man. He looked back at me, grinning.

'You've taken that, too,' I said.

He held out his hand and there was my watch lying in his palm. 'Nice bit of stuff, this,' he said. 'Superior quality. Eighteen-carat gold. Easy to flog, too. It's never any trouble gettin' rid of quality goods.'

'I'd like it back, if you don't mind,' I said rather huffily.

He placed the watch carefully on the leather tray in front of him. 'I wouldn't nick anything from you, guv'nor,' he said. 'You're my pal. You're giving me a lift.'

'I'm glad to hear it,' I said.

'All I'm doin' is answerin' your questions,' he went on. 'You asked me what I did for a livin' and I'm showin' you.'

'What else have you got of mine?'

He smiled again, and now he started to take from the pocket of his jacket one thing after another that belonged to me – my driving licence, a keyring with four keys on it, some pound notes, a few coins, a letter from my publishers, my diary, a stubby old pencil, a cigarette lighter, and last of all, a beautiful sapphire ring with pearls around it belonging to my wife. I was taking the ring up to the jeweller in London because one of the pearls was missing.

'Now *there's* another lovely piece of goods,' he said, turning the ring over in his fingers. 'That's eighteenth century, if I'm not mistaken, from the reign of King George the Third.'

'You're right,' I said impressed. 'You're absolutely right.'

He put the ring on the leather tray with the other items.

'So you're a pickpocket,' I said.

'I don't like that word,' he answered. 'It's a coarse and vulgar word. Pickpockets is coarse and vulgar people who only do easy little amateur jobs. They lift money from blind old ladies.'

'What do you call yourself, then?'

'Me? I'm a fingersmith. I'm a professional fingersmith.' He spoke the words solemnly and proudly, as though he were telling me he was the President of the Royal College of Surgeons or the Archbishop of Canterbury.

'I've never heard that word before,' I said. 'Did you invent it?'

'Of course I didn't invent it,' he replied. 'It's the name given to them who's risen to the very top of the profession. You've 'eard of a goldsmith and a silversmith, for instance. They're experts with gold and silver. I'm an expert with my fingers, so I'm a fingersmith.'

'It must be an interesting job.'

'It's a marvellous job,' he answered. 'It's lovely.'

'And that's why you go to the races?'

'Race meetings is easy meat,' he said. 'You just stand around after the race, watchin' for the lucky ones to queue up and draw their money. And when you see someone collectin' a big bundle of notes, you simply follows after 'im and 'elps youself. But don't get me wrong, guv'nor. I never takes nothin' from a loser. Nor from poor people neither. I only go after them as can afford it, the winners and the rich.'

'That's very thoughtful of you,' I said. 'How often do you get caught?'

'Caught?' he cried disgusted. '*Me* get caught! It's only pickpockets get caught. Fingersmiths never. Listen, I could take the false teeth out of your mouth if I wanted to and you wouldn't even catch me!'

'I don't have false teeth,' I said.

'I know you don't,' he answered. 'Otherwise I'd 'ave 'ad 'em out long ago!'

I believed him. Those long slim fingers of his seemed able to do anything.

We drove on for a while without talking.

'That policeman's going to check up on you pretty thoroughly,' I said. 'Doesn't that worry you a bit?'

'Nobody's checkin' up on me,' he said.

'Of course they are. He's got your name and address written down most carefully in his black book.'

The man gave me another of his sly, ratty little smiles. 'Ah,' he said. 'So 'ee 'as. But I'll bet 'ee ain't got it all written down in 'is memory as well. I've never known a copper yet with a decent memory as well. Some of 'em can't even remember their own names.'

'What's memory got to do with it?' I asked. 'It's written down in his book, isn't it?'

'Yes, guv'nor, it is. But the trouble is, 'ee's lost the book. 'Ee's lost both books, the one with my name in it *and* the one with yours.'

In the long delicate fingers of his right hand, the man was holding up in triumph the two books he had taken from the policeman's pockets. 'Easiest job I ever done,' he announced proudly.

I nearly swerved the car into a milktruck, I was so excited.

'That copper's got nothin' on either of us now,' he said.

'You're a genius!' I cried.

' 'Ee's got no names, no addresses, no car number, no nothin', ' he said.

'You're brilliant!'

'I think you'd better pull in off this main road as soon as possible,' he said. 'Then we'd better build a little bonfire and burn these books.'

'You're a fantastic fellow,' I exclaimed.

'Thank you, guv'nor,' he said. 'It's always nice to be appreciated.'

Roald Dahl

Liam O'Flaherty

Liam O'Flaherty was born in 1897 in the Aran Islands off County Galway, Southern Ireland. He was brought up in a Gaelic-speaking family and community, and was educated at Rockwell College, Black Rock College and then at the University of Dublin. He was intended for the priesthood, but finding that his real interest was in a military career, he left university in 1915 and joined the Irish Guards. He served in Belgium during the First World War, but was shell shocked and discharged in 1917. He returned to Dublin where he became involved with the Republican cause during the Civil War.

In 1918 he went to work in London, first in a brewery, and then on the stage, the latter without success. Eventually, he joined a ship bound for Rio de Janeiro as a trimmer. He began writing in 1921, rejecting his nautical experiences as subject matter for his fiction; instead he set his stories either in the Aran Islands or in Dublin.

His first novel, *Thy Neighbour's Wife*, was published in 1923. He also published three volumes of his memoirs, *Two Years* (1930), *I Went to Russia* (1931) and *Shame the Devil* (1934). Some of his novels, including *The Informer* and *The Puritan* have been dramatized; however, he is perhaps best known for his short stories.

Liam O'Flaherty remained unmarried and lived mainly in Dublin, with a cottage on his native Aran. He died in Dublin in 1984.

The Sniper

The long June twilight faded into night. Dublin lay enveloped in darkness, but for the dim light of the moon, that shone through fleecy clouds, casting a pale light as of approaching dawn over the streets and the dark waters of the Liffey. Around the beleaguered Four Courts the heavy guns roared. Here and there through the city machine guns and rifles broke the silence of the night, spasmodically, like dogs barking on lone farms. Republicans and Free States were waging civil war.

On a rooftop near O'Connel Bridge, a Republican sniper lay watching. Beside him lay his rifle and over his shoulders were slung a pair of field glasses. His face was the face of a student — thin and ascetic, but his eyes had the cold gleam of the fanatic. They were deep and thoughtful, the eyes of a man who is used to looking at death.

He was eating a sandwich hungrily. He had eaten nothing since morning. He had been too excited to eat. He finished the sandwich, and taking a flask of whiskey from his pocket, he took a short draught. Then he returned the flask to his pocket. He paused for a moment, considering whether he should risk a smoke. It was dangerous. The flash might be seen in the darkness and there were enemies watching. He decided to take the risk. Placing a cigarette between his lips, he struck a match, inhaled the smoke hurriedly and put out the light. Almost immediately, a bullet flattened itself against the parapet of the roof. The sniper took another whiff and put out the cigarette. Then he swore softly and crawled away to the left.

Cautiously he raised himself and peered over the parapet. There was a flash and a bullet whizzed over his head. He dropped immediately. He had seen the flash. It came from the opposite side of the street.

He rolled over the roof to a chimney stack in the rear, and slowly drew himself up behind it, until his eyes were level with the top of the parapet. There was nothing to be seen — just the dim outline of the opposite housetop against the blue sky. His enemy was under cover.

Just then an armoured car came across the bridge and advanced slowly up the street. It stopped on the opposite side of the street fifty yards ahead. The sniper could hear the dull panting of the motor. His heart beat fast r. It was an enemy car. He wanted to fire, but he knew it was useless. His bullets would never pierce the steel that covered the grey monster.

Then round the corner of a side-street came an old woman, her head covered by a tattered shawl. She began to talk to the man in the turret of the car. She was pointing to the roof where the sniper lay. An informer.

The turret opened. A man's head and shoulders appeared, looking towards the sniper. The sniper raised his rifle and fired. The head fell heavily on the turret wall. The woman darted toward the side-street. The sniper fired again. The woman whirled round and fell with a shriek into the gutter.

Suddenly from the opposite roof a shot rang out and the sniper dropped his rifle with a curse. The rifle clattered to the roof. The sniper thought the noise would wake the dead. He stopped to pick the rifle up. He couldn't lift it. His forearm was dead. 'Christ,' he muttered. 'I'm hit.'

Dropping flat on to the roof, he crawled back to the parapet. With his left hand he felt the injured right forearm. The blood was oozing through the sleeve of his coat. There was no pain — just a deadened sensation, as if the arm had been cut off.

Quickly he drew his knife from his pocket, opened it on the breastwork of the parapet and ripped open the sleeve. There was a small hole where the bullet had entered. On the other side there was no hole. The bullet had lodged in the bone. It must have fractured it. He bent the arm below the wound. The arm bent back easily. He ground his teeth to overcome the pain.

Then, taking out his field dressing, he ripped open the packet with his knife. He broke the neck of the iodine bottle and let the bitter fluid drip into the wound. A paroxysm of pain swept through him. He placed the cotton wadding over the wound and wrapped the dressing over it. He tied the end with his teeth.

Then he lay still against the parapet, and closing his eyes, he made an effort of will to overcome the pain.

In the street beneath all was still. The armoured car had retired speedily over the bridge, with the machine gunner's head hanging lifeless over the turret. The woman's corpse lay still in the gutter.

The sniper lay for a long time nursing his wounded arm and planning escape. Morning must not find him wounded on the roof. The enemy on the opposite roof covered his escape. He must kill that enemy and he could not use his rifle. He had only a revolver to do it. Then he thought of a plan.

Taking off his cap, he placed it over the muzzle of his rifle. Then he pushed the rifle slowly upwards over the parapet, until the cap was visible from the opposite side of the street. Almost immediately there was a report, and a bullet pierced the centre of the cap. The sniper slanted the rifle forward. The cap slipped down into the street. Then, catching the rifle in the middle, the sniper dropped his left hand over the roof and let it hang, lifelessly. After a few moments he let the rifle drop to the street. Then he sank to the roof, dragging his hand with him.

Crawling quickly to the left, he peered up at the corner of the roof. His ruse had succeeded. The other sniper seeing the cap and rifle fall, thought that he had killed his man. He was now standing before a row of chimney pots, looking across, with his head clearly silhouetted against the western sky.

The Republican sniper smiled and lifted his revolver above the edge of the parapet. The distance was about fifty yards — a hard shot in the dim light, and his right arm was paining him like a thousand devils. He took a steady aim. His hand trembled with eagerness. Pressing his lips together, he took a deep breath through his nostrils and fired. He was almost deafened with the report and his arm shook with the recoil.

Then, when the smoke cleared, he peered across and uttered a cry of joy. His enemy had been hit. He was reeling over the parapet in his death agony. He struggled to keep his feet, but he was slowly falling forward, as if in a dream. The rifle fell from his grasp, hit the parapet, fell over, bounded off the pole of the barber's shop beneath and then clattered on to the pavement.

Then the dying man on the roof crumpled up and fell forward. The body turned over and over in space and hit the ground with a dull thud. Then it lay still.

The sniper looked at his enemy falling and he shuddered. The lust of battle died in him. He became bitten by remorse. The sweat stood out in beads on his forehead. Weakened by his wound and the long summer day of fasting and watching on the roof, he revolted from the sight of the shattered mass of his dead enemy. His teeth chattered. He began to gibber to himself, cursing the war, cursing himself, cursing everybody.

He looked at the smoking revolver in his hand and with an oath he hurled it to the roof at his feet. The revolver went off with the concussion, and the bullet whizzed past the sniper's head. He was frightened back to his senses by the shock. His nerves steadied. The cloud of fear scattered from his mind and he laughed.

Taking the whiskey flask from his pocket, he emptied it at a draught. He felt reckless under the influence of the spirits. He decided to leave the roof and look for his company commander to report. Everywhere around was quiet. There was not much danger in going through the streets. He picked up his revolver and put it in his pocket. Then he crawled down through the skylight to the house underneath.

When the sniper reached the laneway on the street level, he felt a sudden curiosity as to the identity of the enemy sniper whom he had killed. He decided that he was a good shot whoever he was. He wondered if he knew him. Perhaps he had been in his own company before the split in the army. He decided to risk going over to have a look at him. He peered around the corner into O'Connell Street. In the upper part of the street there was heavy firing, but around here all was quiet.

The sniper darted across the street. A machine gun tore up the ground around him with a hail of bullets, but he escaped. He threw himself face downwards beside the corpse. The machine gun stopped.

Then the sniper turned over the dead body and looked into his brother's face.

Liam O'Flaherty

Doris Lessing

Doris Lessing was born in Khermanshah, Persia (now Iran) in 1919, of British parents. When she was five the family moved to a farm in Southern Rhodesia (now Zimbabwe). She left school at fifteen and worked as a nursemaid and then as a shorthand typist and a telephone operator in Salisbury.

Before leaving Africa for England in 1949, she had married twice and had become involved in radical politics. She took her youngest child with her and the manuscript for her first novel, *The Grass is Singing*, which was published in 1950. This was followed by five novels collectively entitled, *Children of Violence*, published between 1952 and 1969. Her writing was well-received and she went on to write further novels, short stories and non-fiction. He best known book is perhaps *The Golden Notebook*, published in 1962, which is seen as a great landmark by the Women's Movement.

Her concern for politics, the changing role of women and her awareness of the possibility of catastrophe are all issues reflected in her writing.

Doris Lessing's most recent work includes a collection of novels, *Canopus in Argos: Archives*, which have been described as 'space fiction', and her latest book, the disturbing story of *The Fifth Child*.

Flight

Above the old man's head was the dovecote, a tall wire-netted shelf on stilts, full of strutting, preening birds. The sunlight broke on their grey breasts into small rainbows. His ears were lulled by their crooning, his hands stretched up towards his favourite, a homing pigeon, a young plump-bodied bird which stood still when it saw him and cocked a shrewd bright eye.

'Pretty, pretty, pretty,' he said, as he grasped the bird and drew it down, feeling the cold coral claws tighten around his finger. Content, he rested the bird lightly on his chest, and leaned against a tree, gazing out beyond the dovecote into the landscape of a late afternoon. In folds and hollows of sunlight and shade, the dark red soil, which was broken into great dusty clods, stretched wide to a tall horizon. Trees marked the course of the valley; a stream of rich green grass the road.

His eyes travelled homewards along this road until he saw his granddaughter swinging on the gate underneath a frangipani tree. Her hair fell down her back in a wave of sunlight, and her long bare legs repeated the angles of the frangipani stems, bare, shining-brown stems among patterns of pale blossoms.

She was gazing past the pink flowers, past the railway cottage where they lived, along the road to the village.

His mood shifted. He deliberately held out his wrist for the bird to take flight, and caught it again at the moment it spread its wings. He felt the plump shape strive and strain under his fingers; and, in sudden access of troubled spite, shut the bird into a small box and fastened the bolt. 'Now you stay there,' he muttered; and turned his back on the shelf of birds. He moved warily along the hedge, stalking his granddaughter, who was now looped over the gate, her head loose on her arms, singing. The light happy sound mingled with the crooning of the birds, and his anger mounted.

'Hey!' he shouted; saw her jump, look back, and abandon the gate. Her eyes veiled themselves, and she said in a pert neutral voice: 'Hullo, Grandad.' Politely she moved towards him, after a lingering backward glance at the road.

'Waiting for Steven, hey?' he said, his fingers curling like claws into his palm.

'Any objection?' she asked lightly, refusing to look at him.

He confronted her, his eyes narrowed, shoulders hunched, tight in a hard knot of pain which included the preening birds, the sunlight, the flowers. He said: 'Think you're old enough to go courting, hey?'

The girl tossed her head at the old-fashioned phrase and sulked, 'Oh, Grandad!'

'Think you want to leave home, hey? Think you can go running around the fields at night?'

Her smile made him see her, as he had every evening of this warm end-of-summer month, swinging hand in hand along the road to the village with that red-handed, red-throated, violent-bodied youth, the son of the postmaster. Misery went to his head and he shouted angrily: 'I'll tell your mother!'

'Tell away!' she said, laughing, and went back to the gate.

He heard her singing, for him to hear:

> *'I've got you under my skin,*
> *'I've got you deep in the heart of . . .'*

'Rubbish,' he shouted. 'Rubbish. Impudent little bit of rubbish!'

Growling under his breath he turned towards the dovecote, which was his refuge from the house he shared with his daughter and her husband and their children. But now the house would be empty. Gone all the young girls with their laughter and their squabbling and their teasing. He would be left; uncherished and alone, with that square-fronted, calm-eyed woman, his daughter.

He stooped, muttering, before the dovecote, resenting the absorbed cooing birds.

From the gate the girl shouted: 'Go and tell! Go on, what are you waiting for?'

Obstinately he made his way to the house, with quick, pathetic persistent glances of appeal back at her. But she never looked around. Her defiant but anxious young body stung him into love and repentance. He stopped. 'But I never meant . . .' he muttered, waiting for her to turn and run to him. 'I didn't mean . . .'

She did not turn. She had forgotten him. Along the road came the young man Steven, with something in his hand. A present for her? The old man stiffened as he watched the gate swing back, and the couple embrace. In the brittle shadows of the frangipani tree his granddaughter, his darling, lay in the arms of the postmaster's son, and her hair flowed back over his shoulder.

'I see you!' shouted the old man spitefully. They did not move. He stumped into the little whitewashed house, hearing the wooden veranda creak angrily under his feet. His daughter was sewing in the front room, threading a needle held to the light.

He stopped again, looking back into the garden. The couple were now sauntering among the bushes, laughing. As he watched he saw the girl escape from the youth with a sudden mischievous movement, and run off through the flowers with him in pursuit. He heard shouts, laughter, a scream, silence.

'But it's not like that at all,' he muttered miserably. 'It's not like that. Why can't you see? Running and giggling, and kissing and kissing. You'll come to something quite different.'

He looked at his daughter with sardonic hatred, hating himself. They were caught and finished, both of them, but the girl was still running free.

'Can't you *see*?' he demanded of his invisible granddaughter, who was at that moment lying in the thick green grass with the postmaster's son.

His daughter looked at him and her eyebrows went up in tired forbearance.

'Put your birds to bed?' she asked, humouring him.

'Lucy,' he said urgently. 'Lucy . . .'

'Well, what is it now?'

'She's in the garden with Steven.'

'Now you just sit down and have your tea.'

He stumped his feet alternatively, thump, thump, on the hollow wooden floor and shouted: 'She'll marry him. I'm telling you, she'll be marrying him next!'

His daughter rose swiftly, brought him a cup, set him a plate.

'I don't want any tea. I don't want it, I tell you.'

'Now, now,' she crooned. 'What's wrong with it? Why not?'

'She's eighteen. Eighteen!'

'I was married at seventeen and I never regretted it.'

'Liar,' he said. 'Liar. Then you should regret it. Why do you make your girls marry? It's you who do it. What do you do it for? Why?'

'The other three have done fine. They've three fine husbands. Why not Alice?'

'She's the last,' he mourned. 'Can't we keep her a bit longer?'

'Come, now, Dad. She'll be down the road, that's all. She'll be here every day to see you.'

'But it's not the same.' He thought of the other three girls, transformed inside a few months from charming petulant spoiled children into serious young matrons.

'You never did like it when we married,' she said. 'Why not? Every time, it's the same. When I got married you made me feel like it was something wrong. And my girls the same. You get them all crying and miserable the way you go on. Leave Alice alone. She's happy.' She sighed, letting her eyes linger on the sunlit garden. 'She'll marry next month. There's no reason to wait.'

'You've said they can marry?' he said incredulously.

'Yes, Dad, why not?' she said coldly, and took up her sewing.

His eyes stung, and he went out on to the veranda. Wet spread down over his chin and he took out a handkerchief and mopped his whole face. The garden was empty.

From around the corner came the young couple; but their faces were no longer set against him. On the wrist of the postmaster's son balanced a young pigeon, the light gleaming on its breast.

'For me?' said the old man, letting the drops shake off his chin. 'For me?'

'Do you like it?' The girl grabbed his hand and swung on it. 'It's for you, Grandad. Steven brought it for you.' They hung about him, affectionate, concerned, trying to charm away his wet eyes and his misery. They took his arms and directed him to the shelf of birds, one on each side, enclosing him, petting him, saying wordlessly that nothing would be changed, nothing could change, and that they would be with him always. The bird was proof of it, they said, from their lying happy eyes, as they thrust it on him. 'There, Grandad, it's yours. It's for you.'

They watched him as he held it on his wrist, stroking its soft, sun-warmed back, watching the wings lift and balance.

'You must shut it up for a bit,' said the girl intimately. 'Until it knows this is its home.'

'Teach your grandmother to suck eggs,' growled the old man.

Released by his half-deliberate anger, they fell back, laughing at him. 'We're glad you like it.' They moved off, now serious and full of purpose, to the gate, where they hung, backs to him, talking quietly. More than anything could, their grown-up seriousness shut him out, making him alone; also, it quietened him, took the sting out of their tumbling like puppies on the grass. They had forgotten him again. Well, so they should, the old man reassured himself, feeling his throat clotted with tears, his lips trembling. He held the new bird to his face, for the caress of its silken feathers. Then he shut it in a box and took out his favourite.

'*Now* you can go,' he said aloud. He held it poised, ready for flight, while he looked down the garden towards the boy and the girl. Then, clenched in the pain of loss, he lifted the bird on his wrist, and watched it soar. A whirr and a spatter of wings, and a cloud of birds rose into the evening from the dovecote.

At the gate Alice and Steven forgot their talk and watched the birds.

On the veranda, that woman, his daughter, stood gazing, her eyes shaded with a hand that still held her sewing.

It seemed to the old man that the whole afternoon had stilled to watch his gesture of self-command, that even the leaves of the trees had stopped shaking.

Dry-eyed and calm, he let his hands fall to his sides and stood erect, staring up into the sky.

The cloud of shining silver birds flew up and up, with a shrill cleaving of wings, over the dark ploughed land and the darker belts of trees and the bright folds of grass, until they floated high in the sunlight, like a cloud of motes of dust.

They wheeled in a wide circle, tilting their wings so there was flash after flash of light, and one after another they dropped from the sunshine of the upper sky to shadow, one after another, returning to the shadowed earth over trees and grass and field, returning to the valley and the shelter of night.

The garden was all a fluster and a flurry of returning birds. Then silence, and the sky was empty.

The old man turned, slowly, taking his time; he lifted his eyes to smile proudly down the garden at his granddaughter. She was staring at him. She did not smile. She was wide-eyed, and pale in the cold shadow, and he saw the tears run shivering off her face.

Doris Lessing

Frank O'Connor

Frank O'Connor was born Michael Francis O'Donovan in 1903 in Cork, Southern Ireland. He attended the Christian Brothers School, although he spent a lot of time educating himself, learning to speak Gaelic and immersing himself in Gaelic poetry, music and legend. At the age of twelve he began to put together a volume of his collected works.

During the Civil War he fought on the side of the Republic and was imprisoned for his actions in 1923. He read extensively while in prison and learnt several languages. Later he worked as a librarian in Cork where he began to write, initially in Gaelic. His first collection of stories in English, *Guests of the Nation*, was published in 1931, after which new collections appeared regularly and were well-received.

During the 1930s O'Connor went to work in Dublin where W.B. Yeats, an admirer of his work, persuaded him to become the director of the Abbey Theatre. He wrote several plays including *The Invincibles* (1937), *In The Train* (1937) and *Moses' Rock* (1938). However, he resigned from his job in 1958 following quarrels about censorship, and went to the USA, where he spent the rest of his life. He lived in Brooklyn with his American wife, two sons and two daughters, but made frequent visits back to Ireland, travelling around the country by bicycle.

O'Connor's work is characterized by a vivid realism which relies upon a close observation of provincial lower and middle class life in Ireland. He died in March 1966.

My Oedipus Complex

Father was in the army all through the war – the First War, I mean – so, up to the age of five, I never saw much of him, and what I saw did not worry me. Sometimes I woke and there was a big figure in khaki peering down at me in the candlelight. Sometimes in the early morning I heard the slamming of the front door and the clatter of nailed boots down the cobbles of the lane. These were Father's entrances and exits. Like Santa Claus he came and went mysteriously.

In fact, I rather liked his visits, though it was an uncomfortable squeeze between Mother and him when I got into the big bed in the early morning. He smoked, which gave him a pleasant musty smell, and shaved, an operation of astounding interest. Each time he left a trail of souvenirs – model tanks and Gurkha knives with handles made of bullet cases, and German helmets and cap badges and button-sticks, and all sorts of military equipment – carefully stowed away in a long box on top of the wardrobe, in case they ever came in handy. There was a bit of the magpie about Father; he expected everything to come in handy. When his back was turned, Mother let me get a chair and rummage through his treasures. She didn't seem to think so highly of them as he did.

The war was the most peaceful period of my life. The window of my attic faced south-east. My mother had curtained it, but that had small effect. I always woke with the first light and, with all the responsibilities of the previous day melted, feeling myself rather like the sun, ready to illumine and rejoice. Life never seemed so simple and clear and full of possibilities as then. I put my feet out from under the clothes – I called them Mrs Left and Mrs Right – and invented dramatic situations for them in which they discussed the problems of the day. At least Mrs Right did; she was very demonstrative, but I hadn't the same control of Mrs Left, so she mostly contented herself with nodding agreement.

They discussed what Mother and I should do during the day, what Santa Claus should give a fellow for Christmas, and what steps should be taken to brighten the home. There was that little matter of the baby, for instance. Mother and I could never agree about that. Ours was the only house in the terrace without a new baby, and Mother said we couldn't afford one till Father came back from the war because they cost seventeen and six. That showed how simple she was. The Geneys up the road had a baby, and everyone knew they couldn't afford seventeen and six. It was probably a cheap baby, and Mother wanted something really good, but I felt she was too exclusive. The Geneys' baby would have done us fine.

Having settled my plans for the day, I got up, put a chair under the attic window, and lifted the frame high enough to stick out my head. The window overlooked the front gardens of the terrace behind ours, and beyond these it looked over a deep valley to the tall, red-brick houses terraced up the opposite hillside, which were all still in shadow, while those at our side of the valley were all lit up, though with long strange shadows that made them seem unfamiliar; rigid and painted.

After that I went into Mother's room and climbed into the big bed. She woke and I began to tell her of my schemes. By this time, though I never seem to have noticed it, I was petrified in my nightshirt, and I thawed as I talked until, the last frost melted, I fell asleep beside her and woke again only when I heard her below in the kitchen, making the breakfast.

After breakfast we went into town; heard Mass at St Augustine's and said a prayer for Father, and did the shopping. If the afternoon was fine we either went for a walk in the country or a visit to Mother's great friend in the convent, Mother St Dominic. Mother had them all praying for Father, and every night, going to bed, I asked God to send him back safe from the war to us. Little, indeed, did I know what I was praying for!

One morning I got into the big bed, and there, sure enough, was Father in his usual Santa Claus manner, but later, instead of uniform, he put on his best blue suit, and Mother was as pleased as anything. I saw nothing to be pleased about, because, out of uniform, Father was altogether less interesting, but she only beamed, and explained that our prayers had been answered, and off we went to Mass to thank God for having brought Father safely home.

167

The irony of it! That very day when he came in to dinner he took off his boots and put on his slippers, donned the dirty old cap he wore about the house to save him from colds, crossed his legs, and began to talk gravely to Mother, who looked anxious. Naturally, I disliked her looking anxious, because it destroyed her good looks, so I interrupted him.

'Just a moment, Larry!' she said gently.

This was only what she said when we had boring visitors, so I attached no importance to it and went on talking.

'Do be quiet, Larry!' she said impatiently. 'Don't you hear me talking to Daddy?'

This was the first time I had heard those ominous words, 'talking to Daddy', and I couldn't help feeling that if this was how God answered prayers, he couldn't listen to them very attentively.

'Why are you talking to Daddy?' I asked with as great a show of indifference as I could muster.

'Because Daddy and I have business to discuss. Now don't interrupt again!'

In the afternoon, at Mother's request, Father took me for a walk. This time we went into town instead of out to the country, and I thought at first, in my usual optimistic way, that it might be an improvement. It was nothing of the sort. Father and I had quite different notions of a walk in town. He had no proper interest in trams, ships, and horses, and the only thing that seemed to divert him was talking to fellows as old as himself. When I wanted to stop he simply went on, dragging me behind him by the hand; when he wanted to stop I had no alternative but to do the same. I noticed that it seemed to be a sign that he wanted to stop for a long time whenever he leaned against a wall. The second time I saw him do it I got wild. He seemed to be settling himself forever. I pulled him by the coat and trousers, but, unlike Mother who, if you were too persistent, got into a wax and said: 'Larry, if you don't behave yourself, I'll give you a good slap,' Father had an extraordinary capacity for amiable inattention. I sized him up and wondered would I cry, but he seemed to be too remote to be annoyed even by that. Really, it was like going for a walk with a mountain! He either ignored the wrenching and pummelling entirely, or else glanced down with a grin of amusement from his peak. I had never met anyone so absorbed in himself as he seemed.

At teatime, 'talking to Daddy' began again, complicated this time by the fact that he had an evening paper, and every few minutes he put it down and told Mother something new out of it. I felt this was foul play. Man for man, I was prepared to compete with him any time for Mother's attention, but when he had it all made up for him by other people it left me no chance. Several times I tried to change the subject without success.

'You must be quiet while Daddy is reading, Larry,' Mother said impatiently.

It was clear that she either genuinely liked talking to Father better than talking to me, or else that he had some terrible hold on her which made her afraid to admit the truth.

'Mummy,' I said that night when she was tucking me up, 'do you think if I prayed hard God would send Daddy back to the war?'

She seemed to think about that for a moment.

'No, dear,' she said with a smile. 'I don't think he would.'

'Why wouldn't he, Mummy?'

'Because there isn't a war any longer, dear.'

'But, Mummy, couldn't God make another war, if He liked?'

'He wouldn't like to, dear. It's not God who makes wars, but bad people.'

'Oh!' I said.

I was disappointed about that. I began to think that God wasn't quite what he was cracked up to be.

Next morning I woke at my usual hour, feeling like a bottle of champagne. I put out my feet and invented a long conversation in which Mrs Right talked of the trouble she had with her own father till she put him in the Home. I didn't quite know what the Home was but it sounded the right place for Father. Then I got my chair and stuck my head out of the attic window. Dawn was just breaking, with a guilty air that made me feel I had caught it in the act. My head bursting with stories and schemes, I stumbled in next door, and in the half-darkness scrambled into the big bed. There was no room at Mother's side so I had to get between her and Father. For the time being I had forgotten about him, and for several minutes I sat bolt upright, racking my brains to know what I could do with him. He was taking up more than his fair share of the bed, and I couldn't get comfortable, so I gave him several kicks that made him grunt and stretch. He made room all right, though. Mother waked and felt for me. I settled back comfortably in the warmth of the bed with my thumb in my mouth.

'Mummy!' I hummed, loudly and contentedly.

'Sssh! dear,' she whispered. 'Don't wake Daddy!'

This was a new development, which threatened to be even more serious than 'talking to Daddy'. Life without my early-morning conferences was unthinkable.

'Why?' I asked severely.

'Because poor Daddy is tired.'

This seemed to me a quite inadequate reason, and I was sickened by the sentimentality of her 'poor Daddy'. I never liked that sort of gush; it always struck me as insincere.

'Oh!' I said lightly. Then in the most winning tone: 'Do you know where I want to go with you today, Mummy?'

'No, dear,' she sighed.

'I want to go down the Glen and fish for thornybacks with my new net, and then I want to go out to the Fox and Hounds, and –'

'Don't-wake-Daddy!' she hissed angrily, clapping her hand across my mouth.

But it was too late. He was awake, or nearly so. He grunted and reached for the matches. Then he stared incredulously at his watch.

'Like a cup of tea, dear?' asked Mother in a meek, hushed voice I had never heard her use before. It sounded almost as though she were afraid.

'Tea?' he exclaimed indignantly. 'Do you know what the time is?'

'And after that I want to go up the Rathcooney Road,' I said loudly, afraid I'd forget something in all those interruptions.

'Go to sleep at once, Larry!' she said sharply.

I began to snivel. I couldn't concentrate, the way that pair went on, and smothering my early-morning schemes was like burying a family from the cradle.

Father said nothing, but lit his pipe and sucked it, looking out into the shadows without minding Mother or me. I knew he was mad. Every time I made a remark Mother hushed me irritably. I was mortified. I felt it wasn't fair; there was even something sinister in it. Every time I had pointed out to her the waste of making two beds when we could both sleep in one, she had told me it was healthier like that, and now here was this man, this stranger, sleeping with her without the least regard for her health!

He got up early and made tea, but though he brought Mother a cup he brought none for me.

'Mummy,' I shouted, 'I want a cup of tea, too.'

'Yes, dear,' she said patiently. 'You can drink from Mummy's saucer.'

That settled it. Either Father or I would have to leave the house. I didn't want to drink from Mother's saucer; I wanted to be treated as an equal in my own home, so, just to spite her, I drank it all and left none for her. She took that quietly, too.

But that night when she was putting me to bed she said gently:

'Larry, I want you to promise me something.'

'What is it?' I asked.

'Not to come in and disturb poor Daddy in the morning. Promise?'

'Poor Daddy' again! I was becoming suspicious of everything involving that quite impossible man.

'Why?' I asked.

'Because poor Daddy is worried and tired and he doesn't sleep well.'

'Why doesn't he, Mummy?'

'Well, you know, don't you, that while he was at the war Mummy got the pennies from the Post Office?'

'From Miss MacCarthy?'

'That's right. But now, you see, Miss MacCarthy hasn't any more pennies, so Daddy must go out and find us some. You know what would happen if he couldn't?'

'No,' I said, 'tell us.'

'Well, I think we might have to go out and beg for them like the poor old woman on Fridays. We wouldn't like that, would we?'

'No,' I agreed. 'We wouldn't.'

'So you'll promise not to come in and wake him?'

'Promise.'

Mind you, I meant that. I knew pennies were a serious matter, and I was all against having to go out and beg like the old woman on Fridays. Mother laid out all my toys in a complete ring round the bed so that, whatever way I got out, I was bound to fall over one of them.

When I woke I remembered my promise all right. I got up and sat on the floor and played – for hours, it seemed to me. Then I got my chair and looked out the attic window for more hours. I wished it was time for Father to wake; I wished someone would make me a cup of tea. I didn't feel in the least like the sun; instead, I was bored and so very, very cold! I simply longed for the warmth and depth of the big featherbed.

At last I could stand it no longer. I went into the next room. As there was still no room at Mother's side I climbed over her and she woke with a start.

'Larry,' she whispered, gripping my arm very tightly, 'what did you promise?'

'But I did, Mummy,' I wailed, caught in the very act. 'I was quiet for ever so long.'

'Oh, dear, and you're perished!' she said sadly, feeling me all over. 'Now, if I let you stay will you promise not to talk?'

'But I want to talk, Mummy,' I wailed.

'That has nothing to do with it,' she said with a firmness that was new to me. 'Daddy wants to sleep. Now, do you understand that?'

I understood it only too well. I wanted to talk, he wanted to sleep – whose house was it, anyway?

'Mummy,' I said with equal firmness, 'I think it would be healthier for Daddy to sleep in his own bed.'

That seemed to stagger her, because she said nothing for a while.

'Now, once for all,' she went on, 'you're to be perfectly quiet or go back to your own bed. Which is it to be?'

The injustice of it got me down. I had convicted her out of her own mouth of inconsistency and unreasonableness, and she hadn't even attempted to reply. Full of spite, I gave Father a kick, which she didn't notice but which made him grunt and open his eyes in alarm.

'What time is it?' he asked in a panic-stricken voice, not looking at Mother but at the door, as if he saw someone there.

'It's early yet,' she replied soothingly. 'It's only the child. Go to sleep again. . .   Now, Larry,' she added, getting out of bed, 'you've wakened Daddy and you must go back.'

This time, for all her quiet air, I knew she meant it, and knew that my principal rights and privileges were as good as lost unless I asserted them at once. As she lifted me, I gave a screech, enough to wake the dead, not to mind Father. He groaned.

'That damn child! Doesn't he ever sleep?'

'It's only a habit, dear,' she said quietly, though I could see she was vexed.

'Well, it's time he got out of it,' shouted Father, beginning to heave in the bed. He suddenly gathered all the bedclothes about him, turned to the wall, and then looked back over his shoulder with nothing showing only two small, spiteful, dark eyes. The man looked very wicked.

To open the bedroom door, Mother had to let me down, and I broke free and dashed for the farthest corner, screeching. Father sat bolt upright in bed.

'Shut up, you little puppy!' he said in a choking voice.

I was so astonished that I stopped screeching. Never, never had anyone spoken to me in that tone before. I looked at him incredulously and saw his face convulsed with rage. It was only then that I fully realized how God had codded me, listening to my prayers for the safe return of this monster.

'Shut up, you!' I bawled, beside myself.

'What's that you said?' shouted Father, making a wild leap out of the bed.

'Mick, Mick!' cried Mother. 'Don't you see the child isn't used to you?'

'I see he's better fed than taught,' snarled Father, waving his arms wildly. 'He wants his bottom smacked.'

All his previous shouting was as nothing to these obscene words referring to my person. They really made my blood boil.

'Smack your own!' I screamed hysterically. 'Smack your own! Shut up! Shut up!'

At this he lost his patience and let fly at me. He did it with the lack of conviction you'd expect of a man under Mother's horrified eyes, and it ended up as a mere tap, but the sheer indignity of being struck at all by a stranger, a total stranger who had cajoled his way back from the war into our big bed as a result of my innocent intercession, made me completely dotty. I shrieked and shrieked, and danced in my bare feet, and Father, looking awkward and hairy in nothing but a short grey army shirt, glared down at me like a mountain out for murder. I think it must have been then that I realized he was jealous too. And there stood Mother in her nightdress, looking as if her heart was broken between us. I hoped she felt as she looked. It seemed to me that she deserved it all.

From that morning out my life was a hell. Father and I were enemies, open and avowed. We conducted a series of skirmishes against one another, he trying to steal my time with Mother and I his. When she was sitting on my bed, telling me a story, he took to looking for some pair of old boots which he alleged he had left behind him at the beginning of the war. While he talked to Mother I played loudly with my toys to show my total lack of concern. He created a terrible scene one evening when he came in from work and found me at his box, playing with his regimental badges, Gurkha knives, and button-sticks. Mother got up and took the box from me.

'You mustn't play with Daddy's toys unless he lets you, Larry,' she said severely. 'Daddy doesn't play with yours.'

For some reason Father looked at her as if she had struck him and then turned away with a scowl.

'Those are not toys,' he growled, taking down the box again to see had I lifted anything. 'Some of those curios are very rare and valuable.'

But as time went on I saw more and more how he managed to alienate Mother and me. What made it worse was that I couldn't grasp his method or see what attraction he had for Mother. In every possible way he was less winning than I. He had a common accent and made noises at his tea. I thought for a while that it might be the newspapers she was interested in, so I made up bits of news of my own to read to her. Then I thought it might be the smoking, which I personally thought attractive, and took his pipes and went round the house dribbling into them till he caught me. I even made noises at my tea, but Mother only told me I was disgusting. It all seemed to hinge round that unhealthy habit of sleeping together, so I made a point of dropping into their bedroom and nosing round, talking to myself, so that they wouldn't know I was watching them, but they were never up to anything that I could see. In the end it beat me. It seemed to depend on being grown-up and giving people rings, and I realized I'd have to wait.

But at the same time I wanted him to see that I was only waiting, not giving up the fight. One evening when he was being particularly obnoxious, chattering away well above my head, I let him have it.

'Mummy,' I said, 'do you know what I'm going to do when I grow up?'

'No, dear,' she replied. 'What?'

'I'm going to marry you,' I said quietly.

Father gave a great guffaw out of him, but he didn't take me in. I knew it must only be pretence. And Mother, in spite of everything, was pleased. I felt she was probably relieved to know that one day Father's hold on her would be broken.

'Won't that be nice?' she said with a smile.

'It'll be very nice,' I said confidently. 'Because we're going to have lots and lots of babies.'

'That's right, dear,' she said placidly. 'I think we'll have one soon, and then you'll have plenty of company.'

I was no end pleased about that because it showed that in spite of the way she gave in to Father she still considered my wishes. Besides, it would put the Geneys in their place.

It didn't turn out like that, though. To begin with, she was very preoccupied – I supposed about where she would get the seventeen and six – and though Father took to staying out late in the evenings it did me no particular good. She stopped taking me for walks, became as touchy as blazes, and smacked me for nothing at all. Sometimes I wished I'd never mentioned the confounded baby – I seemed to have a genius for bringing calamity on myself.

And calamity it was! Sonny arrived in the most appalling hullabaloo – even that much he couldn't do without a fuss – and from the first moment I disliked him. He was a difficult child – so far as I was concerned he was always difficult – and demanded far too much attention. Mother was simply silly about him, and couldn't see when he was only showing off. As company he was worse than useless. He slept all day, and I had to go round the house on tiptoe to avoid waking him. It wasn't any longer a question of not waking Father. The slogan now was 'Don't-wake-Sonny!' I couldn't understand why the child wouldn't sleep at the proper time, so whenever Mother's back was turned I woke him. Sometimes to keep him awake I pinched him as well. Mother caught me at it one day and gave me a most unmerciful flaking.

One evening, when Father was coming in from work, I was playing trains in the front garden. I let on not to notice him; instead, I pretended to be talking to myself, and said in a loud voice: 'If another bloody baby comes into this house, I'm going out.'

Father stopped dead and looked at me over his shoulder.

'What's that you said?' he asked sternly.

'I was only talking to myself,' I replied, trying to conceal my panic. 'It's private.'

He turned and went in without a word. Mind you, I intended it as a solemn warning, but its effect was quite different. Father started being quite nice to me. I could understand that, of course. Mother was quite sickening about Sonny. Even at mealtimes she'd get up and gawk at him in the cradle with an idiotic smile, and tell Father to do the same. He was always polite about it, but he looked so puzzled you could see he didn't know what she was talking about. He complained of the way Sonny cried at night, but she only got cross and said that Sonny never cried except when there was something up with him –

which was a flaming lie, because Sonny never had anything up with him, and only cried for attention. It was really painful to see how simple-minded she was. Father wasn't attractive, but he had a fine intelligence. He saw through Sonny, and now he knew that I saw through him as well.

One night I woke with a start. There was someone beside me in the bed. For one wild moment I felt sure it must be Mother, having come to her senses and left Father for good, but then I heard Sonny in convulsions in the next room, and Mother saying: 'There! There! There!' and I knew it wasn't she. It was Father. He was lying beside me, wide awake, breathing hard and apparently as mad as hell.

After a while it came to me what he was mad about. It was his turn now. After turning me out of the big bed, he had been turned out himself. Mother had no consideration now for anyone but that poisonous pup, Sonny. I couldn't help feeling sorry for Father. I had been through it all myself, and even at that age I was magnanimous. I began to stroke him down and say: 'There! There!' He wasn't exactly responsive.

'Aren't you asleep either?' he snarled.

'Ah, come on and put your arm around us, can't you?' I said, and he did, in a sort of way. Gingerly, I suppose, is how you'd describe it. He was very bony but better than nothing.

At Christmas he went out of his way to buy me a really nice model railway.

Frank O'Connor